The Presence of the Past: The Public Museum of Grand Rapids at 150

The Presence of the Past

The Public Museum of Grand Rapids at 150

BY JULIE CHRISTIANSON STIVERS

Public Museum of Grand Rapids

The Presence of the Past: The Public Museum
of Grand Rapids at 150

by Julie Christianson Stivers

© 2004 The Public Museum of Grand Rapids

ISBN: 0-9666524-1-x

All inquiries should be directed to:
The Public Museum of Grand Rapids
272 Pearl Street NW
Grand Rapids, MI 49504-5371
WWW.GRMUSEUM.ORG

First Edition

Thomas Kachadurian: Art Director
Veronica Kandl: Project Coordinator

Cover Photographs: see page 131
Back Cover Photograph: see page 25

Printed in Canada

Public Museum of Grand Rapids

Time present and time past
Are both perhaps present in time future,
And time future contained in time past.

—T.S. Eliot, *Four Quartets,* Burnt Norton, 1935

Table of Contents

OPPOSITE: The formal entryway at Voigt House, built in 1895-6, features an elegant stairway with hand-turned oak spindles and a brass light fixture original to the house. The turn-of-the-century fixture lights with both trustworthy gas and 'new-fangled' electrical power. Dozens of exotic oriental rugs, along with a splendid collection of family treasures, are displayed at the home, which is now preserved by the Public Museum of Grand Rapids.

BELOW: A slab of hemlock blazed with surveyor's marks made in the U.S. Government's original survey of northern Kent County in 1837. Donated to the Public Museum in 1947, it was exhibited for decades in the old Museum's Discovery & Exploration Hall. It will return to public view in the exhibition *X Marks the Spot* at Van Andel Museum Center.

Preface

The Public Museum of Grand Rapids has flourished for 150 years because it has continually evolved to stay relevant to its changing and growing community. As we celebrate a long history built on the dedication and vision of its many founders, we are also celebrating the tenth anniversary of the Public Museum's primary exhibition facility—the architecturally significant Van Andel Museum Center.

When John Ball and his fellow citizens began the Public Museum in 1854, they informally set in place some founding principles that continue to define the institution and which provide direction to the present day. Core among these is the idea that the Public Museum is an educational institution dedicated to lifelong informal learning for everyone—from children to elders. It is oriented towards its utility for our citizens and visitors, is publicly responsive, and is useful, practical and even necessary for a healthy community. Focused on collecting material culture, artifacts of local history, and noteworthy natural history and scientific specimens, the Museum has consistently relied on a rich base of scientific, ethnographic, anthropological, and historical treasures as tools of insight and inquiry to be used in the pursuit of knowledge. These collections did not originate with the passion of a few, but instead have been assembled with the active participation of thousands of individual donors who felt compelled to save our region's patrimony for the benefit of future generations.

As we celebrate the Public Museum's sesquicentennial, volunteers, staff, and board members realize that we have not so much arrived at a destination, as at a pause on a journey of accomplishment that will continue for at least another 150 years. In 2005 as we labor to complete permanent exhibitions in Van Andel Museum Center, prepare to open the Community Archives & Research Center, and work to reach community consensus for the preservation and access of the 2000-year-old Norton Mounds National Historical Landmark, the Museum's staff felt that undertaking a published history to assess progress would be appropriate. We invited a superb writer who is also an insightful, well-respected commentator on West Michigan's cultural life to delve into our institutional archives and interview dozens of people in order to pen a narrative history of her own design. Julie Christianson Stivers has teamed with Michigan book designer and photographer Thomas Kachadurian to produce a beautifully illustrated chronicle of the Public Museum's past. Together they have married prose and photography to create an artistic composition—a snapshot in time that documents the activities and growth of the institution in an entertaining and illuminating manner that moves skillfully between chronology and recurring themes. Especially interesting in the book are the featured tales and stories of the many personalities who have supported the Museum and worked passionately on its behalf.

I invite you to savor this rich chronicle of a cherished community institution with the hope that it inspires you to continue to support the Public Museum and to use its resources and collections to better place yourself in your community, nation and world.

Dedication

This chronicle of Michigan's first and oldest general museum is dedicated to all of its thousands of workers and employees, both paid and unpaid, who labored to advance their Public Museum for 150 years. Their work ensured that the natural history and cultural patrimony of Grand Rapids and West Michigan was kept, preserved, and made available for use by the many for the common good.

However, throughout these many years, the involvement of several individuals achieved a level of passion and engagement bordering on obsession. Their work conceived of the institution, guided it, molded its personality, and ensured its ongoing relevance. They were and are by no means alone, and I would risk neglecting the accomplishments of many others of note were not their stories and accomplishments detailed in this narrative.

This history of the Public Museum of Grand Rapids, Michigan is therefore also dedicated with the special thanks of a grateful community to the following leaders:

- John Ball, trustee, our legendary founder and explorer, active 1854-1884
- George Wickwire Smith, trustee, our inquisitive, youthful sustainer, active 1865-1869
- Frank L. DuMond, director, our visionary builder, active 1923-ca. 1970s
- Norma Raby, education curator, our tireless educator, active ca. 1930-1981
- Weldon D. Frankforter, director, our advocate for community engagement, active 1962-present
- Marilyn Merdzinski, collections manager, our preserver of heritage, active 1977-present
- Steele A. Taylor, trustee, our tireless champion, active 1976-present
- Jay Van Andel, patron, our generous benefactor, active 1982-present
- Mary Esther Lee, assistant director, our tenacious manager of planning, active 1972-present

— Timothy J. Chester, Director & CEO
Public Museum of Grand Rapids

Public Museum of Grand Rapids Staff 2004

1. The Early Years: 1854—1932

The origins of The Public Museum of Grand Rapids lie within two 19th-century associations whose ideals still resonate in the mission of the Museum 150 years later.

The Grand Rapids Lyceum of Natural History was established in 1854 by a group of civic leaders, inspired by a movement sweeping the country. Followers of the Lyceum Movement believed that education, in the form of libraries, museums, lectures and discussions, and public schools, could help right the illnesses of society and preserve democracy.

In the fall of 1865, four boys decided, after a day of tramping through the woods and gathering specimens south of the city, to organize the Grand Rapids Scientific Club. It was an exciting time to be a curious student—remote parts of the planet were being mapped, new species of animals, plants and insects were being discovered (Charles Darwin's *On the Origin of Species by Natural Selection* had been published only six years earlier), and new sciences were being developed.

When the two organizations merged in 1868 to become the Kent Scientific Institute, the stage was set for a public museum that remains driven, 150 years later, by the ideals of educational enthusiasm and community service.

The Grand Rapids Lyceum of Natural History

In 1854, Grand Rapids was a young community. Incorporated as a city just four years earlier, the former trading post was attracting a steady stream of settlers from the east. John Ball came to Michigan as an agent, or 'land-looker', for New York investors. Educated at Dartmouth College, he was a teacher and world-traveller with wide interests and many talents. He arrived in Grand Rapids in 1836 and remained an active and revered member of the community until his death at age 90 in 1884.

John Ball and James H. McKee, Land Agents and Attorneys-at-Law, had an office on the second floor of a building on Monroe Street in downtown Grand Rapids. In the fall of 1854, their friends, carpenter and conchologist A.O. Currier (who had, in his younger days, been a curator at a museum in Troy, New York), and W.G. Henry, who operated a drug-

JOHN BALL,
Attorney and Counsellor at Law,
GRAND RAPIDS, MICH.
Land Agency and Collection Business promptly attended to in Kent, and adjoining counties.
REFERS TO
Messrs. John Steward, Jr. & Co., N. York. | Messrs. L. O. Wilson & Co., N. York.
" H. E. Dibblee & Co. | G. Hathaway, Esq. "
" Grinnell & Minturn. | Geo. S. Seymour, Esq. Laporte, Ind.

store in the same building, dropped by for a visit. The men shared an interest in science, and, as Currier later remembered in a speech on the history of the organization, John Ball posed the question, "Why not have a Lyceum of Natural History in Grand Rapids?

The group moved quickly. In the archives of the Public Museum of Grand Rapids is a record book that begins: "Saturday Evening, Nov. 25th, 1854. Agreeable to Notice, a number of gentleman met at the Union School House for the purpose of organizing a Scientific Association. On motion John Ball was chosen Chairman, and C.E. Fuller, Secretary." Other civic leaders named as officers were Wright L. Coffinberry, an amateur archaeologist and City Engineer, whose name the local archaeological society still bears, and Charles Shepard as Vice Presidents, Franklin Everett, headmaster of the Grand Rapids Academy, as Corresponding Secretary, and Curators A.O. Currier, W.H. DeCamp and M.S. Littlefield, with E.W. Chesebro as librarian. Several members offered to loan their "cabinets of Natural Curiosities" to the society, and the by-laws outlined a wide scope of interests, including lectures and discussions, a museum, and a library.

BELOW LEFT: **A portrait of John Ball, who came to Grand Rapids in 1836 as a 'land-looker,' to find property for investors in the east. The portrait of John Ball, and one of his wife, Mary Webster Ball, were given to the Museum in 1950 by the widow of his grandson, Mrs. Floss Ball, and now hang in the Board Room at Van Andel Museum Center.**

OPPOSITE: **A writing case used by John Ball on an expedition in 1832 which crossed the Great Plains to the Pacific Northwest, given to the Public Museum in 1943 by his daughter, Mrs. Myron H. Hopkins.**

MONROE ST.

The Lyceum met in the city's first high school at Lyon and Ransom, and the principal (and Lyceum librarian), E.W. Chesebro, was given permission to use the collections for instructional purposes. The group also tried a downtown location, but by 1859 attendance and interest were waning as the nation moved inexorably toward Civil War. On January 23, 1860, the concluding minutes in the record book of the Grand Rapids Lyceum of Natural History read: "Meeting called to order. A few members present. Just as we were about to adjourn the cry of fire was raised, which proved to be the store of Porter S. Sligh, which was entirely destroyed. Adjourned one week."

A cry of fire, indeed. 90,000 soldiers from Michigan fought in the Civil War and more than 14,000 gave their lives. It would be years before the ideals of community service and education would again be taken up in Grand Rapids.

The Grand Rapids Scientific Club

"Now, what I want is, Facts. Teach these boys and girls nothing but Facts. Facts alone are wanted in life. Plant nothing else, and root out everything else. You can only form the minds of reasoning animals upon Facts: nothing else will ever be of any service to them. This is the principle on which I bring up my own children, and this is the principle on which I bring up these children. Stick to facts, sir!"

So said Mr. Thomas Gradgrind, in Charles Dickens' novel, *Hard Times*, published in 1854. Dickens saw the development of science and technology in Victorian England as a threat to wonder and the realms of the imagination, and a stifling influence on eager young minds.

But to four young high school students in Grand Rapids, Michigan, in the summer of 1865, new ideas about science and and nature were part of a resurgence of educational enthusiasm that would bring the fledgling Museum back to life.

The story of four young boys collecting specimens in the woods—a blue racer snake, a stag beetle, a piece of chain coral, a bunch of wild daisies—and returning from their outing to organize a scientific club, is a favorite Public Museum history vignette. Charles Garfield, Hertel S. Fitch, J. Frederick Baars, Jr., and George Wickwire Smith established the Grand Rapids Scientific Club in September with a constitution, by-laws, and officers.

New members were soon added, and the stated principal goal of collecting specimens proceeded at a great rate. The club first met in the home on Lyon Street where George W. Smith and his father boarded, and as they grew rented rooms downtown. In 1866 they published a monthly paper, and the group's meetings began to attract a public following.

The club was assisted by Professor E.A. Strong, Superintendent of Schools, who encouraged the boys to correspond with other scientific societies and to trade specimens with them. Professor Strong also was instrumental in bringing the members of the Scientific Club, which they had re-named the Kent Institute in 1867 to reflect their county-wide scope, together with the older men of the Grand Rapids Lyceum, whose collections had been stored in the homes of members since 1860.

On January 2, 1868, Articles of Association of the Kent Scientific Institute were signed by John Ball, A.O. Currier, A.L. Chubb, and

James H. McKee of the Lyceum of Natural History, and by G.Wickwire Smith, S.H. Winchester, William H. McKee, L.G. Winchester, Theo. B. Wilson, Frank W. Ball, and John Matthison, representing the Kent Institute. John Ball was elected president.

Kent Scientific Institute & Museum

The merger of the two organizations put the museum on the path of growth, reflecting the growth of the city and of the nation, and the increasing importance of bringing together a widely diverse society into something distinctively American. Between 1860 and 1870, the

LEFT: The articles of association that joined the Lyceum of Natural History and the Grand Rapids Scientific Club. The signatures on the constitution of the new Kent Scientific Institute (ABOVE), including John Ball and George Wickwire Smith, are specimens of interest to any scholar of early Grand Rapids history.

OPPOSITE TOP: A stereopticon image of early downtown Grand Rapids, showing arches erected to celebrate the U.S. centennial in 1876.

FAR LEFT: Charles Garfield, the first president of the Grand Rapids Scientific Club, became a successful banker and legislator, and also was a noted conservationist. As chair of the Board of Trade (an early predecessor to the Chamber of Commerce), he led a campaign to plant thousands of trees along the streets of Grand Rapids in the 1890s, a legacy that lives on in the shady, green city along with his old family farm on Burton Street bordering Plaster Creek, where the young members of the Scientific Club found inspiration. A bust of Garfield, at left, was presented to the Public Museum by a local bank in the early 1950s.

Members of the Grand Rapids Scientific Club: Although the names of Ball and McKee indicate a certain connection between club members and older scientifically minded men in the community, and Charles W. Garfield would go on to a successful career as a banker and was a well-known conservationist (Garfield Park stands as a monument to his philanthropy), it was George Wickwire Smith who was acknowledged as the heart and soul of the Scientific Club. Nicknamed "The Professor," he was the first graduate of the Commercial College in Grand Rapids and an editor for a Grand Rapids newspaper at age 19.

Smith died tragically young in 1869, at age 21. His obituary describes him as "wholly devoid of affectation, modest and retiring in disposition . . . a favorite with his teachers . . . his classmates regarded him with love and admiration." (Readers of Louisa May Alcott will immediately recognize the beloved, bright, but doomed, boy.) In an article following his death from "lung fever," the young man's last moments are described by his father, the Rev. Dr. C.B. Smith. When asked whether he preferred to be buried in the family's grounds in Oneida, New York, or in Grand Rapids, he is said to have replied, "I don't care, father, bury me where there are the most butterflies." In the Fulton Street Cemetery in Grand Rapids, not 100 feet from the enormous boulder that marks the final resting place of John Ball, is the plot purchased by the Rev. C.B. Smith in 1870. A modest stone marker bears the initials G.W.S.

MEMBERS OF THE GRAND RAPIDS SCIENTIFIC CLUB WHO GATHERED MUCH OF PRESENT COLLECTION OF KENT SCIENTIFIC MUSEUM

Standing, from left to right — Henry J. Carr, Lorenzo G. Winchester, Eugene F. Sawyer, Theodore Wilson, Frank W. Ball.

Sitting, from left to right — William H. McKee, Geo. Wickwire Smith, Chas. W. Garfield, Hertel S. Fitch.

population of Grand Rapids roughly doubled, from around 8000 to over 16,000. Trains and telephones were connecting the city with the rest of the world at a speed previously unbelievable. The post-Civil War expansion of industry and commerce was mirrored by a burst of scientific and intellectual activity. Great museums were founded in New York, Boston, Philadelphia.

In the early years of the 20th century, a report on museums compiled by the Director of the Museum of Charleston, and published by the U.S. Bureau of Education, numbered some 600 institutions nationwide which assumed the name museum. According to John Cotton Dana, founder and first director of The Newark Museum, and one of the most influential writers about museums in America, only about 80 of those so enumerated, however, could properly be called "live." He defined his term, in a 1917 essay, as possessing certain fundamentals: "a home, collections properly so called, an income, and most important of all these essentials, such activities as may fairly be supposed to produce beneficial effects in their respective communities."

The Kent Scientific Institute was slowly working its way to "life." Housed at Central High School under an 1881 agreement with the Board of Education, the collection grew rapidly, according to a history of the institution written by Professor E. A. Strong, Director of the Institute's Museum for many years. Strong wrote that the KSI collection "became known to those interested in such matters throughout the land." Albert Baxter, in his 1891 *History of Grand Rapids*, wrote that the Kent Scientific Institute "has grown to be among the finest scientific collections in the West." Income, as ever was and ever shall be, fluctuated. Everyone involved with the Institute served without salary.

But there was no question about "beneficial effects." The collections were used by the principal and teachers at the school, and a number of scientific projects were undertaken. In a report published in June 1902 in *The Helios*, the yearbook of Central High School, A.J. Volland, Director of the Museum from 1898-1900 and subsequently a member of the joint committee formed by KSI and the Board of Education to run the Museum, wrote, "Our object has not been to make a museum of freaks and curiosities, but to collect material that would enable students in our schools and the public generally to turn the leaves of the great book of nature— the first volume that God ever wrote—to read its pages understandingly and enjoyably, and to prepare them to perform every duty of life and fill every station they may be called upon to occupy more satisfactorily to themselves and more beneficially to the rest of mankind."

High ideals, and a reference to the fact that two types of museums had developed in 19th-century America. The first, a public institution providing educational and wholesome activities; the second, established for commercial purposes and dedicated solely to entertainment, popularly called the 'dime museum.' Best known among these was perhaps Phineas T. Barnum's museum of 'living human curiosities,' which grossed $400,000 in 1871. Grand Rapids seems to have had its own sideshow museum. Photographs from 1870 depict a building on Pearl Street labeled Museum, often mistaken for an early home of the Public Museum. It is in fact Crane's Museum of Freaks, Snakes, and Whiskered Ladies, located on the second floor of Houseman & May Clothing Store.

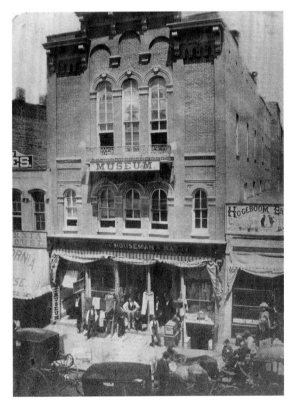

Entering a New Century

The years just before the turn of the century were exciting ones for the newly emerging institution. Excavations of area Indian mounds led by Wright L. Coffinberrry, City Engineer and one of the founders of the Lyceum, resulted in

LEFT: **Crane's Museum, mentioned in Albert Baxter's 1891** *History of the City of Grand Rapids*, **and identified as Crane's Museum of Freaks, Snakes, and Whiskered Ladies in a later publication. An 1870 City Directory lists Elliott H. Crane as proprietor of Crane's Museum at 14 Pearl, but by 1874 he is listed simply as Professor Crane, taxidermist. Little else has been published about the establishment, but Public Museum records show that on July 10, 1917, the Kent Scientific Institute purchased a substantial number of objects from the E.H. Crane Estate, including many Native American artifacts that are still in the collections of the Public Museum of Grand Rapids.**

INSET RIGHT: Emma J. Cole, in a photograph from the faculty page of *The Delphian 1896*, the yearbook of Central High School. Cole was somewhat overlooked in the history of the city until 1994, when as part of a Women's History Month project she was profiled in a play commissioned to celebrate the achievements of Grand Rapids women. *Invisible Journeys*, by local playwright Jean Reed Bahle, resulted in a new look at four women who played an important role in the city's history.

ABOVE: Pages from Emma Cole's book *Grand Rapids Flora*, published 1901.

an impressive collection of "relics," which the Institute was invited to exhibit at the Centennial Exposition in Philadelphia in 1876. Although security was tight during the exposition, the exhibition case was broken into the night before it was to close, and the objects stolen. Attempts to determine exactly what was lost, and speculation about the whereabouts of the looted relics, continue to this day.

It is also during this era when names of women begin appearing in the archives of the Public Museum. Mrs. E.L. Briggs was named a Vice President of the Institute in 1881, and in 1882 the name of Mrs. G.C. Fitch appears. But the woman most associated with the early years of the museum is Emma J. Cole.

Emma Cole was born in 1845 in Midland, Ohio and sometime after that her family established a farm near Lowell in Michigan. She

attended Cornell University, and in 1882 became a teacher in the Grand Rapids Public Schools. For 26 years she taught botany at

EMMA J. COLE.

Central High School, with breaks for travel throughout Europe and the U.S., where she did work at institutions including Harvard and Berkeley, and the Arnold Arboretum in Boston. In 1901, she published *Grand Rapids Flora*, detailing her work identifying "plants growing without cultivation" around the city. The Kent Scientific Institute paid her room and board expenses while she mounted and identified botanical specimens she had collected and donated to the institution, and in 1900 she was named a Vice President of the organization. Emma Cole died in 1910, leaving a variety of bequests to churches and institutions to encourage the appreciation of the area's native flora.

The turn of the century marked a difficult time for relations between the Board of Education and Kent Scientific Institute. Grand Rapids was growing rapidly. In 1880 its population was 32,000; ten years later it was 60,000, and by 1900 it had grown to 88,000. Increased school enrollment caused the Institute's collection to be shifted around and eventually much of it was placed in storage. By February, 1900, secretary C.A. Whittemore recorded in the minutes, "Attendance lightest in history of KSI. Some meetings only one person present beside the secretary." At the end of 1900, the Institute agreed to donate its museum and library to the Board, in return for a home for the collection and a full-time curator. In 1901, the Board hired Professor Herbert E. Sargent, Curator of the Museum of Natural History at the University of Michigan, as a part-time consultant to analyze the collection and make suggestions for its exhibition. At their January 1903 meeting, the

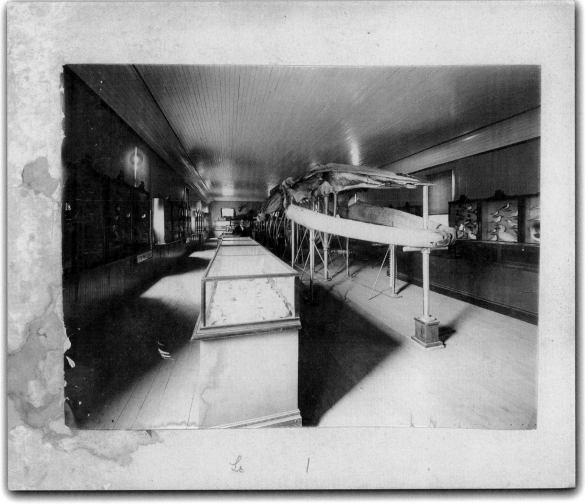

ABOVE: Built in the 1880s by wealthy lumberman D.P. Clay, the three-story residence on Jefferson Street that became the first permanent home of the Kent Scientific Museum was purchased by the Board of Education from Mathilda Howlett of Grand Haven in 1903 for $22,000. It was opened to the public on January 7, 1904. At the rear of the lot stood a two-story frame building used as a carriage house and stable, with living quarters upstairs. The main residence contained about 7500 sq. ft., the outbuilding 4500.

LEFT: In 1906 a long, low "barn" was built along the north side of the carriage house to contain the 70-foot skeleton of a whale, which would become one of the Museum's most beloved icons. In 1917, the Museum Board rented the vacant Hughart house across the street on the corner of Weston and Jefferson. The three-story yellow brick residence was fitted with cases and many exhibits transferred to what became known as "The Annex."

LEFT: Herbert E. Sargent was born in Raymond, New Hampshire in 1864. He was educated at Carleton College and Columbia University, and married Belle Whittemore in 1890. He was on the faculty at the University of Michigan and responsible for the collection of the University's Museum of Natural History from 1898-1903 before coming to Grand Rapids.

Upon his death in 1944, *Grand Rapids Herald* editor Frank M. Sparks wrote that Sargent "knew perhaps as much as any living man" about shells, and "likewise knew a lot about mammals, especially those long extinct." A musk ox fossil he helped to excavate from a swamp near Ravenna in 1904 was thought to be a species new to science, and in honor of Mr. Sargent was named *Bootherium sargenti.* Later the species was found not to be distinctive, but in November 2000, it became part of the *F is for Fossils* section of the *Collecting A to Z* permanent exhibition at Van Andel Museum Center. *Bootherium sargenti,* though probably a female of the species *Bootherium bombifrons,* still has a story to tell.

RIGHT: Dr. E.S. Holmes, President of Kent Scientific Institute, with his camera, ca. 1905.

last part of the 19th century. He was a member of many scientific organizations, and served as president of the Michigan Dental Association, where he was important in establishing the dental school at the University of Michigan.

The elation of Dr. Holmes was matched only by the collecting zeal of Herbert Sargent. The Museum made several significant acquisitions in

the early years of the century. A mastodon skeleton unearthed near Ravenna was acquired in 1904, and in 1905 an enormous whale skeleton was purchased. In 1909 an Egyptian mummy and related artifacts were given to the Museum by Edward A. Lowe. In addition to the acquisition of a large collection of some 200,000 specimens from John Kost of Adrian, Michigan, purchased at the same time as the Howlett property, Curator Sargent pursued collections from far and wide, mining expositions in St. Louis, Jamestown, and many others.

In 1906 the Board of Education decided to turn over responsibility for the Kent Scientific Institute and Museum to the newly created Board of Library Commissioners, which assumed complete control in 1910. On August 29, 1916, the City of Grand Rapids adopted a Charter which created the Board of Art and Museum Commissioners, whose duty was "to have the custody, management and control of

Board of Education reported that an area in the High School was ready for occupation.

After years of procrastination and indecision, however, the Board of Education made a sudden surprise move. At their February meeting they announced the purchase of the Howlett home at the corner of Jefferson and Washington, to be converted into a Museum, and at the March meeting Professor Sargent was hired as full-time Curator at a salary of $1500 per year.

Kent Scientific Museum

"The city is getting a bargain and the Kent Scientific Institute collection will at last be properly housed," said Dr. E.S. Holmes, President of KSI, in an article in the *Grand Rapids Herald.* A local dentist who for more than forty years was a driving force behind the Institute, Holmes was a well-known public figure in the

Although Henry Ward worked diligently to make the kind of improvements in Grand Rapids that he had accomplished in Milwaukee, he felt thwarted at every turn. His diatribes about his difficulties, printed in the Museum's Annual Reports, while distressing, make for guiltily entertaining reading. "The long, painful waiting for an opportunity to attend and the mob condition of pushing, pulling and struggling when the crowd begins to move into the building are factors militating against a receptive mental mood." he wrote, describing the scene at Curator of Education Frank DuMond's popular lectures for children. "The whole thing is wrong; unbecoming a city department; inimical to gentlemanly and ladylike deportment; dangerous to health and to life and limb."

the Museum." On April 1, 1917, The Board of Library Commissioners turned control over to the Board of Art and Museum Commissioners, where it has remained to this day. Charles B. Kelsey was the first President.

Sargent's collecting continued to fill the Museum to bursting. A positive result of his acquisitive nature was the development of a number of portable collections for loan to schools, assembled from duplicate specimens. Temporary exhibits were placed in downtown bank windows, and for many years special Museum displays were an attraction at the annual West Michigan State Fair. An annex was rented across the street from the Museum.

But Sargent began to fall from favor with Board members, who became convinced that he was careless with the collection, and absent from the Museum far too often on collecting ven-

tures. In 1921 the Commission asked him to resign. After an exchange of recriminations, closely covered by the newspapers, his employment was terminated.

Good News & Bad News

In 1922 Henry L. Ward was hired to replace Herbert Sargent. Son of the founder of the renowned Ward's Natural Science Establishment of Rochester, New York, Henry Ward had been Director of the Milwaukee Public Museum for 18 years, during which time a new museum facility had been constructed and the institution's stature greatly increased. At age 57 he had retired to Bellingham, Washington, where he operated a chicken farm. Ward enthusiastically pursued the Grand Rapids position, and immediately after his hiring embarked on an ambi-

tious plan to float a $600,000 bond proposal
to the citizens of the city. The proposal on the
April 1923 election ballot was defeated, but the
City Commission heeded Ward's emphatic and
repeated complaints that nothing could be done
without increased funding, and voted to boost
the Museum's budget by more than 40%.

One of Ward's first steps toward revitalizing
the Museum was to hire a Curator of
Education, Frank L. DuMond. Over the next
four decades, the young Cornell University
graduate would become one of the best-known
and best-loved figures in the history of the
Public Museum.

The popular education and public programming developed by DuMond, and general
improvements in the Museum's exhibitions,
prompted increased appropriations by the City
Commission, and in 1928 the Grand Rapids
Board of Education voted to purchase services
from the Museum for a total of $2500.

But despite the good news, attendance at the
Museum began dropping. Ward renewed his
appeals for a new building, but the response
from the city was unenthusiastic. Ominous sig-
nals of economic decline led the City Commission to begin cutting the Museum's allocation,
and in 1932 they slashed it by 87%. The Board of
Education also reduced its grant, resulting in a
Museum budget that went from $37,500 to
$15,000. The Art & Museum Commission met
in special session to discuss the crisis, and
decided to reduce staff to six. The resignation of
Director Henry L. Ward was accepted. Frank
DuMond was named Acting Director.

RIGHT: On the third floor of Van Andel Museum Center,
which opened in 1994, is a representation of a room
from the Kent Scientific Museum, containing many
artifacts from that era. Through the door can be seen
dioramas recreated from the Jefferson Street building
that opened in 1940. The rooms are part of the
natural history galleries, and were created not only to
remember the Museum's history, but also to examine
changing ideas about museums and exhibitions.

2. Education

I F THE HISTORY of the Public Museum can be compared to a tapestry, education and community service are the warp and weft through which all its activities are woven. And, to stretch the metaphor, like the colored strand woven into all ropes used by the British Navy, education is visible in the Museum's every activity, from collecting and preservation to exhibitions and programming.

When Henry Ward embarked on his plan to rejuvenate and reorganize the Museum, his first step was to hire a Curator of Education. Frank DuMond arrived in October, 1923 with no background in museums, but passionate ideas about education and young people. Trained as a forester at Cornell and Yale, he had been active as a scoutmaster and nature counselor in boys' camps. In a story about DuMond in the *Grand Rapids Herald* upon his arrival, he was confident he knew how to appeal to young boys. "His imagination, active throughout boyhood, is exceptionally fertile in these years," he explained. "Nothing can be too weird, too supernatural, too horrible even, to engage that mind ... by keeping a lap or two ahead of their imaginations I usually succeed in keeping them interested." His ideas would shape and drive the Public Museum for more than four decades. (A

visit to the natural history galleries at Van Andel Museum Center today will reveal that young boys—and girls—still find the weird world of animals, including roundworms, fascinating.)

DuMond had a strong foundation on which to build. The Museum's roots were in the public schools, and with students whose enthusiasm embraced new ideas. But curious minds of all ages have found stimulation and enlightenment through Museum activities spanning its entire history. One of the first meetings of the Grand Rapids Lyceum of Natural History was a public lecture. Professor Franklin Everett spoke in a

OPPOSITE: **Frank DuMond, ca. 1925, with school children assembling at the Kent Scientific Institute for one of his popular Saturday afternoon programs.**

BELOW: **Stereoview card, undated, reads on the back "Beginning of Kent Scientific Museum in Old Central High."** Image courtesy Grand Rapids History & Special Collections Center, Archives, Grand Rapids Public Library.

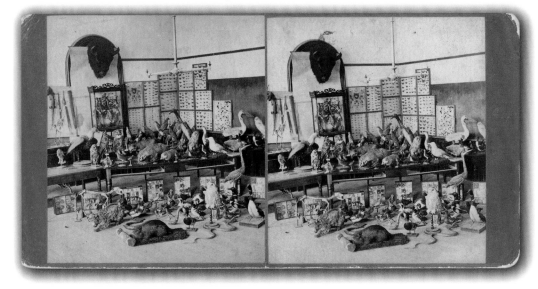

Museum Director Frank DuMond places himself in a piece of 15th-century history donated to the Public Museum by Hollis S. Baker in 1951 (perhaps not now considered best museum practice, but the Director had worked very hard to secure a suit of armor for the Museum's collection). DuMond's background was not in museums. In a 1978 *Grand Rapids Press* article, reporter Gerald Elliott wrote that the Kent Scientific Institute was the first museum DuMond ever visited. He held master's degrees in forestry from Cornell and Yale, and worked summers in sawmills and lumber camps, for the U.S. Forest Service and at Boy Scout camps.

From his arrival in Grand Rapids in 1923 to his retirement in 1965, and beyond, Frank DuMond, known to his friends as Dewey, was an active and tireless community leader. In addition to his remarkable achievements at the Public Museum, he served many organizations as volunteer and board member, including the Historical Society of Michigan, American Red Cross, Grand Rapids Civic Theatre, Salvation Army, Michigan Audubon Society, Izaak Walton League, G.R. Rotary Club, the Saladin Shrine, and many more, several of which distinguished him with a variety of honors and awards. He was a prolific writer, and published many books and articles, including a regular Sunday feature for the *Grand Rapids Herald*. After his retirement, he spent years researching and writing *A Narrative History of the Grand Rapids Public Museum, 1854–1970*, unpublished, but invaluable in the making of this book. Frank DuMond was married to Margaret Thomas in 1926 and they had four children. He died in 1989 at the age of 91.

"special meeting" on February 8, 1855, open to the public. His talk, *The Effect of Water upon the Surface of the Earth*, can be regarded as the first public educational program in the Museum's history. Public lectures, discussions, and publications were an important part of the activities of the Lyceum and the Scientific Club, and have continued through all the incarnations of the Public Museum of Grand Rapids to the present day.

Synergy with Schools

It's not surprising that an institution whose collections were first housed in the city's schools remains closely aligned with the region's educational systems. Even after the Museum moved into its own building in 1904, Herbert Sargent used the enormous collections he amassed to make duplicate specimens available for schools, and began a series of regular lectures both in schoolrooms and at the Museum.

Upon his arrival in 1923, Frank DuMond immediately began meeting with public school teachers to determine their needs. In an improvised auditorium in the Kent Scientific Museum 'Annex,' fitted with 100 folding chairs, he began a series for 4th–8th grades, illustrated by lantern slides. Word spread among the public and private schools and the lectures were soon filled to overflowing. The school loan program also continued, and by 1928, Director Ward reported that among the materials available for in-school programs were 40,000 photographs, 425 bird specimens in boxes, cases of insects, minerals, and textiles. The Board of Education acknowledged the increased instructional value of the Museum's programs by appropriating $2500 in 1928 to purchase its services.

In the decades of the Depression and World War II, DuMond, who became Acting Director in 1932, carried on valiantly while the Museum's budget and staff were cut to almost nothing. Loans to schools, and weekend and evening programs continued, and in 1933 the City of Grand Rapids actually increased the

In 1912, Director Herbert Sargent presented a report at the American Association of Museums conference on "circulating bird cases" the Kent Scientific Museum had adopted the previous year. The Museum continued to make a large number of materials available to schools through its Visual Education Division until 1981.
LEFT: Portable displays of birds, mammals, insects, minerals, shells, and other natural history specimens are stacked in transit to conservation facilities in the new Community Archives and Research Center, 2003.

BELOW: Miss Gladys Carpenter, who had a large following in the early 1920s as host of a local children's radio program, was in charge of the Kent Scientific Museum's Nature Room and gave nature talks in local schools from 1925-28.

Museum's appropriation because it was one of the few institutions offering free education and recreation year-round to the citizens of the city. DuMond was named Director in 1934. Throughout the Depression, he made good use of funding from agencies including the WPA, FERA and NYA to augment the Museum's limited education staff (Depression-era funding is covered in Chapter Four of this book).

After World War II, in a new building and with a new name (events covered elsewhere in this history), the Grand Rapids Public Museum embarked on an educational expansion that matched the soon-to-be overwhelming onslaught of the baby-boom generation. In the mid-1940s, Evelyn Grebel, who had come to the Museum from the City's Recreation Department, began a series of summer programs for vacationing students. Since then thousands of children and their relieved parents have found respite from summer doldrums at the Museum.

The post-war education expansion also was led by Norma Raby, who became supervisor of visual instruction in 1940, and Mary Jane Dockeray, who came to the museum in 1948 as a nature lecturer and became best known as the driving force behind Blandford Nature Center (more about Ms. Dockeray can be found in Chapter Six of this book). In the fall of 1948, 'Teas for Teachers' brought 191 educators to the

ABOVE: Saturday craft classes in the early 1950s.

RIGHT: "Anting in Fulton Park," summer 1960, with Anne Leiber, who was assistant to the director, as well as filling many other roles at the Museum, from the 1960s to her retirement in March 1982.

BELOW: Evelyn Grebel, who directed the Museum's children's programs for more than 25 years beginning in 1944, leads a group on a "Historical Hike" in downtown Grand Rapids in 1962.

Museum to acquaint them with available services. In 1950, the two created slide talks about Michigan coordinated with fourth-grade textbooks written by a committee of local teachers.

Although cooperation with schools and teachers had always been a part of the Museum's educational programs, the relationship between school curriculum and the development of Museum programs grew closer. In 1953, the Museum began publishing *Musette*, a newsletter for teachers. In the mid-1990s, *Musette* began offering information for teachers on direct links between Museum education

programming and the State of Michigan's curriculum requirements. *Musette* was sent to more than 6500 educators in West Michigan during the 2003-4 school year and was accessible through the Museum's web site.

In the 1959-60 school year, the Museum established an expanded Visual Education Department in its new East Building, sending out programs and materials to schools throughout the region until 1981. A van delivered and picked up materials ranging from mounted photographs, films and recordings to objects including mounted birds, animals and historical collections. As the guide-lecture services offered within the

Museum grew, the delivery service was discontinued and more school children were brought to the Museum for hands-on education within the exhibitions, the focus of the Museum's education program today. During the 2003-2004 school year, the Museum was reassessing teacher resource needs for the future and the school loan program.

In 1974, the Board of Education worked closely with the Museum to establish the Blandford Environmental Education Program (BEEP), housed at Blandford Nature Center. Since then, sixth-grade students have used the Nature Center year round as a living textbook for ecology, economics, chemistry, biology and much more, and are actively involved in Nature Center operations and educational programs. Initial interest in BEEP was so strong that a second program at the John Ball Zoo was implemented.

The BEEPs, as they affectionately came to be known, celebrated the 30th anniversary of the program in August of 2003 with a reunion attended by more than 500 former students and teachers.

Blandford also has offered natural and cultural history experiences for students from throughout the West Michigan school systems, bringing thousands of children to the Nature Center and sending naturalists into classrooms.

In 2004, an innovative partnership between the Public Museum, the City of Grand Rapids and the Grand Rapids Public Schools was launched. The Museum agreed to lease Blandford Nature Center to the school district, which had already planned to develop the adjacent C.A. Frost Elementary School into a K-8 environmental education academy. The partnership will allow the schools to expand environmental education programs to many more students from throughout the city.

In 2000, the Museum became part of a pilot project with the Grand Rapids Public Schools and the U.S. Department of Education to establish 21st Century Learning Centers at area middle schools. In the summer of 2003, students from five middle schools spent six weeks at Van Andel Museum Center, researching, designing

LEFT AND ABOVE: Norma Raby with a set of her famous slides near the WPA map of Michigan, 1951, and with Judith Vis, moving the Education Loan Collection to the East Building in January, 1960.

Norma Raby began volunteering at the Kent Scientific Museum at the age of 12. A native of Grand Rapids, she attended the University of Michigan and worked in the botany department of Grand Rapids Junior College. Her entire life was devoted to the Public Museum, however, and she became a paid employee in 1940. In an organization whose history is filled with long, dedicated careers, hers is among the most extensive. She developed a large loan collection of prints, slides, films, exhibitions and other educational aids, traveling throughout the U.S. and abroad to take photographs for the collection. The audio-visual department was eliminated in June, 1981 as part of a drastic city budget cutback, and Norma died in September just weeks after her retirement. For many years the Michigan Museums Association gave annual awards in her name for excellence in museum education.

LEFT: Museum staff members Tom DeFouw and Buryl Mercer Shoults load exhibits into the loan collection van, 1952.

Contemporary education at the Public Museum is multi-sensory and multi-media. FAR RIGHT: Learning to start a fire at Blandford Nature Center, 2000. RIGHT: A young visitor uses a computer station to learn about objects more than 2000 years old in *The Dead Sea Scrolls Discovery Room*, 2003. BELOW: Students work on an exhibition about the history of the Grand Rapids Public Schools during the summer, 2003, with Paula Gangopadhyay, foreground right, who became Curator of Education & Public Programming in 2002.

and building *Project Exhibition—History of Grand Rapids Public Schools*. The project was exhibited at Van Andel Museum Center for several months before traveling to the participating schools.

Paula Gangopadhyay, who became Curator of Education at the Public Museum in October 2002, describes a new relationship for museums and school systems. "Museum education programming is undergoing a paradigm shift," she said in a 2003 interview, "from a supplement to fulfilling curriculum requirements. We provided a MEAP (Michigan Education Assessment Program) literacy enhancement

during the summer of 2003 with the *Read and Connect* program including exhibition labels, vocabulary, speaking, and reading comprehension. We are exploring new roles for the Museum in home schooling, charter schools, college courses, long-distance learning, career pathways."

In February 2003, more than thirty superintendents from the Kent Intermediate School District met at Van Andel Museum Center to discuss the ambitious and ground-breaking educational programs for the exhibition *The Dead Sea Scrolls*. Many Museum records were shattered by the internationally acclaimed exhibition, including attendance from February 16-June 1, 2003 of 235,541. More than 28,000 students came to the Museum in school groups for programs in history, geography, cultures of the world, and more. "*The Dead Sea Scrolls* provided the Museum a platform to explore the potential for programming and reach for new heights of excellence," Paula said. "It was a leap of faith and developed multi-layered programming for all ages and backgrounds."

Timothy J. Chester, who became Director of the Public Museum in 1988, has described the success of educational programming as an example of how the Public Museum has at times followed trends and been "part of the pack," and at times has found itself assuming a national leadership role. "The Public Museum operated primarily in the education mode well past its

time, when it was no longer fashionable for a museum to be defined as an educational institution in the 1960s and '70s," he explained in a 2003 interview. "Now, it finds itself, by virtue of having stayed its course, to be suddenly on the cutting edge of best museum practices. We are reasserting education as our primary mission."

Community Partners

The school systems of West Michigan have not been the Museum's only partners in providing educational services to students throughout the area. In 1963, the Junior League of Grand Rapids established the Grand Rapids Public Museum Guides, a group of 25 trained volunteers who conducted classroom tours through the Museum's exhibitions and developed programs in conjunction with classroom curriculum. The League also purchased a 48-passenger bus to bring school children to the Museum.

In 1969, the guides, now called Docents, became an independent group, part of the

Grand Rapids Museum Association (later the Friends of the Public Museum). In 1976, the Public Museum hosted a national seminar for the American Association for State and Local History. "The Training of Museum Docents" was organized by Curator of Education Kay Zuris and Mary Jane Dockeray, and featured top professionals in museum education as faculty.

The Docentry League became part of the Museum's Education, Public Programming & Visitor Services Department in 2003, and continues to provide an important service to the students of West Michigan and to the Museum. Gina Bivins, who joined the Museum's Collections staff in 1992 and the Education Department in 1996, was a Museum volunteer in the late 1970s and became a Docent in 1981. She remembers that Docent training was rigorous, "for some a little intimidating," she said in a 2003 interview. "But I always felt like I was a member of the staff, expected to be a professional. From the first day we were expected to present the materials and the collections thoughtfully and professionally, and to present

Kay A. Zuris was named the Public Museum's Curator of Education in 1975. A graduate of the University of Missouri and Allegheny College, she had been a curator and director of two institutions in the east before accepting the post in Grand Rapids. For 13 years she built an admired and widely emulated museum education program, and became nationally known for her rigorous and fun docent training programs. In 1986 she began developing new exhibitions for the Museum, and in 1988 was named Assistant Director. Kay retired in 2003, after curating the dream exhibition of her career, *Leagues of Their Own*, a history of Michigan's connections to the All-American Girls Professional Baseball League and the Negro Leagues of the 1940s and '50s.

RIGHT: Kids discover a safe way to view a solar eclipse, 1963.

ourselves in the same way. We work very hard to continue that today. The tours are written to enhance the curriculum, we make it meaningful for teachers."

The Junior League stepped forward again in 1984 with a three-year project to expand the guide-interpreter corps at Blandford Nature Center, funding a part-time coordinator.

Knowledge with a Capital K

When British scientist and adventurer James Smithson somewhat mysteriously left his estate to the fledgling American government in 1829, he wrote that his intent was "an Establishment for the increase & diffusion of Knowledge among men." The idea of museums created for the education of the common citizens, rather than royal or aristocratic institutions, was growing in the new country. In his 2002 book, *Making Museums Matter*, published by the

Smithsonian Institution, noted American writer and museum administrator Stephen Weil describes the development of these ideas in the late 19th century. "Beyond the capacity to elevate the taste and purify the morals of its visitors," he wrote, "the museum was also envisioned by its founders as providing a wholesome alternative to the seamier forms of entertainment."

These ideas were leading to an increase in museum programming not only for schoolchildren, but for citizens of all ages and all walks of life. In an essay titled "The Concept of a Modern Museum," Kent Scientific Museum Director Herbert Sargent wrote in 1920, "No community is intellectually greater than the combined intellect of its constituent members."

Programs for adults and families that were not only educational but entertaining became an important part of the Public Museum's mission. In 1961, Board of Art & Museum

Commissioners President A.W. Hewitt wrote, "The Museum, because of its popular constructive leisure-time programs for children, is a strong deterring force against juvenile delinquency." Ralph B. Baldwin, Commission President in 1964, waxed a little more philosophical. "Little wonder that the modern museum is called 'the University of the Common Man' for it appeals to people of all ages, of all interests and all intellectual backgrounds," he wrote. "Here is the truth as exemplified by the forms created by Nature or fashioned by the skilled hands of Man."

Dr. Baldwin was president of the Grand Rapids Board of Art & Museum Commissioners through most of the 1960s. Head of Oliver Machinery Company, he was a graduate of the University of Michigan who taught at Northwestern University and lectured in astronomy at the Adler Planetarium in Chicago. He was an active volunteer for the Public Museum, assisting in the establishment of the Chaffee Planetarium, and as recently as the summer of 2002 was still publishing internationally recognized theories about scientific matters.

Dr. Baldwin was also the first president of the Grand Rapids Museum Association, a support organization formed in March, 1952. The Museum Association, later called the Friends of the Public Museum, became the source of volunteers and funding for a wide variety of special events, guest speakers, conferences, research projects, film and lecture series, and many other activities to supplement Museum programming. Over the years the group also devised many fundraising ideas, including development of the Museum Shop (now the Curiosity Shop), and was very active in planning and raising funds in the 1980s for the

ABOVE: John Douglas, President of the Museum Association in the 1960s and '70s, served in many volunteer roles at the Public Museum, including presenter of a regular film series in the Museum's Multi-Purpose Room and as a member of the planning committee for a new Museum building. He is leaning against the Museum's calliope truck, a familiar part of local festivals and parades for many years.

ABOVE LEFT: Maridell VanderBaan (left) and Carol Muth, carry the banner for the Friends in the Festival 1989 parade through downtown Grand Rapids, followed by Spike the Dinosaur, promoting the *Dinamation* exhibition at the Public Museum.

BOTTOM LEFT: Members of the media sample an educational activity during *Mysteries of Egypt*, November 1999, with Mannie Gentile, front, Curator of Education from 1990-2000.

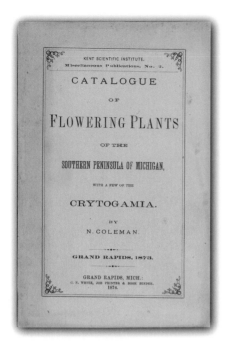

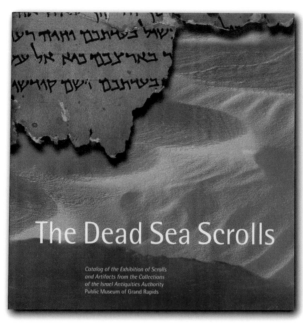

The Dead Sea Scrolls

Catalog of the Exhibition of Scrolls
and Artifacts from the Collections
of the Israel Antiquities Authority
Public Museum of Grand Rapids

Museum publications over the years have played an important role in disseminating research and enhancing the community's learning opportunities.
ABOVE: One of the earliest publications of the Kent Scientific Institute, 1873.
TOP: The catalog of *The Dead Sea Scrolls* exhibition, published by the Public Museum with the Wm. B. Eerdmans Publishing Co. of Grand Rapids and the Israel Antiquities Authority, was a significant contribution to international scholarship.

LEFT: One of a series of seven publications produced by the Museum Association in the late 1970s and early 1980s was *Printing: Impact on Man*.

OPPOSITE PAGE: Trevor and Michael Huisman contemplate the presence of the past at Van Andel Museum Center, December 2003.

Museum's eventual move from its primary facility on Jefferson Avenue to its new riverside location. In 2002, the Friends merged with the Public Museum Foundation of Grand Rapids to become the Public Museum of Grand Rapids Friends Foundation, whose many members are carrying on the work to support the Museum and its programs.

The Museum Association also established the Museum's monthly newsletter for members, *Discoveries*, in 1952, and formed an active and prolific Publications Committee.

Books and other printed materials produced by the Public Museum have played an important role in disseminating research and enhancing the community's lifelong learning opportunities. For the Museum's Victorian-era founders, publications were a connection to scientists and researchers throughout the world. E.A. Strong, Superintendent of Schools and one of the Museum's first movers and shakers, authored a weighty tome, *Notes Upon the Fossil Remains of the Lower Carboniferous Limestone Exposed at Grand Rapids, Michigan*, the first in a series that carried the Kent Scientific Institute imprint. Others included *List of the Shell-Bearing Mollusca of Michigan*, by A.O. Currier, 1868, and *Catalogue of Flowering Plants of the Southern Peninsula of Michigan*, by N.

Coleman, 1873. And the KSI played a major role in supporting Emma Cole's 1901 book, *Grand Rapids Flora*, featured in Chapter One of this book.

In 1976, the Museum Association embarked on another ambitious publications series that resulted in seven projects, covering topics as diverse as the *Calkins Law Office* and *Beads: Their Use by Upper Great Lakes Indians* to *Woodcarvings of the African Makonde* and *Printing: Impact on Man*. Their support has made possible a number of definitive works, including *Greentown Glass* in 1978 and *Grand Rapids Furniture: The Story of America's Furniture City*, in 1998.

Written by Museum Curator of Collections Christian G. Carron, *Grand Rapids Furniture* was the first major history on the subject, and has become a valued resource for scholars and collectors throughout the country (more about the Museum's connection to the furniture industry can be found in Chapter Five). In 2003, the Museum made another significant contribution to international research with the publication of *The Dead Sea Scrolls*. Edited by the exhibition's curator, Ellen Middlebrook Herron, the catalogue has become a highly esteemed reference for new and previous scholarship about the 2000-year-old treasures.

But scholarly research and intellectual inquiry are not the only educational benefits for which the community turns to the Public Museum. Popular movies, entertaining ethnic heritage festivals and events, hands-on arts and crafts, music, dancing, great food and much more fun have long been an important part of the Museum's education programs. From Youth Talent Exhibitions to Garden Clubs, the Museum has served, and continues to serve, a wide variety of community interests, which are featured later in this book.

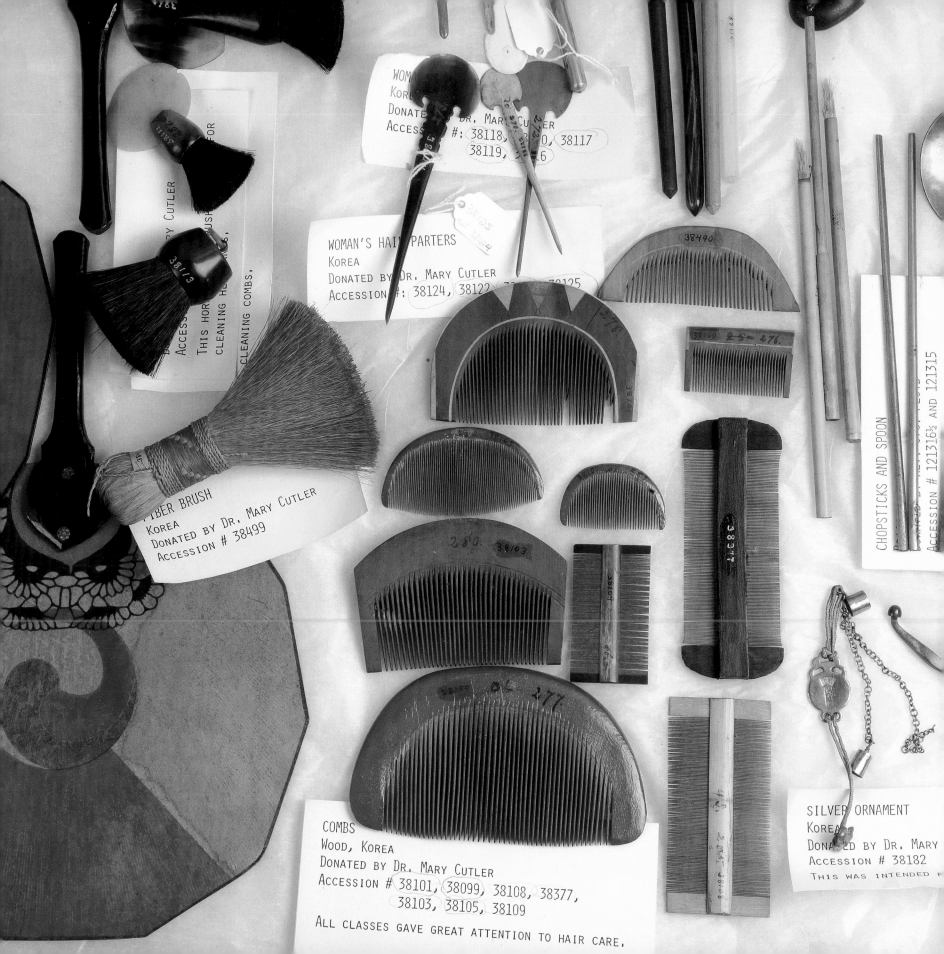

WOMAN'S HAIR PARTERS
Korea
Donated by Dr. Mary Cutler
Accession #: 38118, 38120, 38117
38119, 38116

WOMAN'S HAIR PARTERS
Korea
Donated by Dr. Mary Cutler
Accession #: 38124, 38122, 38123, 38125

FIBER BRUSH
Korea
Donated by Dr. Mary Cutler
Accession # 38499

CHOPSTICKS AND SPOON
Korea
Donated by Dr. Mary Cutler
Accession # 121316½ AND 121315

SILVER ORNAMENT
Korea
Donated by Dr. Mary
Accession # 38182
This was intended f

COMBS
Wood, Korea
Donated by Dr. Mary Cutler
Accession # 38101, 38099, 38108, 38377,
38103, 38105, 38109

ALL CLASSES GAVE GREAT ATTENTION TO HAIR CARE.

This hor
cleaning h
cleaning combs.

3. Citizens of the World

As this book was being written, another part of the celebration of the 150th anniversary of the Public Museum of Grand Rapids was also in the works. A new permanent exhibition at Van Andel Museum Center will explore the history of race and ethnicity in the region, the latest of many projects in the Museum's 150 years that help the people of West Michigan understand ourselves as citizens of the world.

From the first days of the Lyceum, curiosity about the planet drove a collecting zeal that resulted in a mass of preserved flora and fauna flowing into the city from around the world. Missionaries brought cultural treasures back from far corners, and other world travelers made sure that Grand Rapids had its share of marvels from distant places and distant times.

Putting Prejudices Aside

People were naturally drawn to the exotic and unfamiliar (this was, after all, a time when P.T. Barnum exhibited 'A Chinese Family' as a sideshow), but as the nation grew, fueled by immigrants from exactly those faraway places, another interest began to surface.

In the 19th century, a goal of many American museums was to help educate growing immigrant populations. By the turn of the cen-

tury, nearly two-thirds of the population of Grand Rapids had been born in another country, including Ireland, the Netherlands, Germany, Poland, Lithuania, Italy, Scandinavia, Greece, and many others. A large number were drawn by the city's industries, particularly furniture, and settled in ethnic enclaves. In 1911, a massive furniture workers strike racked the city, and prejudices and antagonisms emphasized religious and cultural divisions.

But in 1917, when the U.S. entered the

OPPOSITE AND LEFT: **Dr. Mary Cutler, a Grand Rapids Methodist missionary who spent many years in Korea, brought hundreds of pieces of clothing, art, utensils, and other objects typical of Korean culture back to West Michigan upon her return in the early 20th century, along with dozens of photographs documenting her experiences there. The photos are interesting not only as glimpses of another time and place, but also because many objects that can be seen in the images remain in the collections of the Public Museum.**

The Museum's Egyptian mummy is one of its oldest and most storied artifacts. Purchased in Cairo by Grand Rapids philanthropist Edward Lowe, who was connected to both the Butterworth and Blodgett families, it was donated to the Kent Scientific Museum in 1909. That season's attendance, 54,741, represented a 23% increase over the previous year's stile records, attributed by Director Herbert Sargent to public interest in the mummy, particularly when he bowed to popular demand and unwrapped it in 1910.

The mummy, identified as from the Third Intermediate Period, 22nd Dynasty, 946-722 B.C.E., and its related ancient artifacts were exhibited in the old Kent Scientific Museum, and the later Grand Rapids Public Museum building, until 1994, when they were put into storage for the move to Van Andel Museum Center.

In 1999, as part of the blockbuster exhibition *Mysteries of Egypt*, the mummy again played a role in shattering all previous Museum attendance records. In conjunction with the exhibition, which was organized by the Canadian Museum of Civilization in Ottawa, the Public Museum of Grand Rapids initiated a major project in cooperation with experts at Michigan State University to create forensic facial reconstructions of the mummy's head, and another that was donated to the Museum in 1904 by David W. Kendall. Pictured here, Erik Alexander, Curator of Education and a collections curator at the Museum from 1989-2003, begins the reconstruction process by sending the mummy through MRI scanning at Spectrum Health in Grand Rapids. The results were striking, especially the winsome face of Nakhte-Bastet-Iru, the original mummy.

The mummy, her coffin and cartonnage (detail inset), and the Kendall head now repose on the third floor of Van Andel Museum Center along with scores of Egyptian treasures, some more than 3000 years old. From the Valley of the Nile to a quiet corner overlooking the Grand River half a world away, the mummy continues to whisper her mysterious and spiritual message.

Great War (World War I) in Europe, grievances were put aside as patriotic fervor swept the nation. In Grand Rapids, the Kent Scientific Museum was asked by the Better Homes Exposition committee to organize an exhibition showcasing "people of Grand Rapids who were originally of the various allied nations" (*Grand Rapids Press*, December 1, 1917).

Part of a national association, the local exposition featured model rooms, music, an exhibition of artwork, and special events, and ran from November 28 to December 8 in the Klingman Building. Herbert Sargent gathered objects from local families, including decorated photo frames made by Italian women "of the war zone; and sold by them to raise funds with which to buy food and clothing," and a collection of hand-worked fabric made by a local woman "prior to a subsequent escape from Armenia at the time of the 1915 massacre."

Going Dutch

A Polish Heritage Day and special exhibition also were organized by Director Sargent in 1918 after expanding the Kent Scientific Museum to a house 'annex' across Jefferson Avenue, but little room at either facility was available for further projects. In 1934, however, the intrepid Frank DuMond mounted a special exhibition that was to become a landmark in the Museum's development.

DuMond, who came to the Museum in 1923 as Curator of Education, weathered many storms before being named Acting Director in 1932 and, finally, Director in February 1934. Just two months later, he opened the first in a series of exhibitions that would set the stage for an exploration of ethnic heritage that continues to this day as one of the most important contributions the Public Museum makes to the community life of the region.

The exhibition, featuring the art and culture of the Netherlands, included hundreds of Dutch heirlooms and objects temporarily loaned to the Kent Scientific Museum by area citizens. In conjunction with the month-long exhibition, a pageant titled *Lovers of Liberty* was presented at Central High School, to great acclaim. According to newspaper articles of the time, the Museum was invited by the managing director of the Dutch Exposition at the Chicago World's Fair to present the pageant there, but the logistics of transporting the cast of 350 apparently proved insurmountable.

The Dutch Exhibit was wildly popular with the citizens of Grand Rapids (more than a quarter of whom claimed Dutch heritage), and set new attendance records: 30,000 people in a single month, almost a year's normal attendance. The exhibition and activities were held in a rented garage 'annex' down the street from the Museum's main building, which had been shut down to save money. The Museum had to vacate the garage when the lease expired, and move back to its main building, a 19th-century house. "We had planned to continue with other special exhibits featuring the arts and crafts of additional nationalities," wrote DuMond in 1935, "but this is now impossible due to the physical limitations of the main building."

The popularity of *The Dutch Exhibit* was a springboard for DuMond's campaign for a new museum, detailed in the next chapter of this book.

In the fall of 1949, another community-wide effort organized by the Public Museum brought the Ambassador from the Netherlands to visit the city for the first time, and prompted, three years later, a visit from the country's Queen Juliana. More than 35,000 people attended *The Netherlands Exposition* in 1949, again

breaking Museum records. During the Queen's visit in 1952, the Museum sponsored a contest for costume reproductions representing the provinces of the Netherlands. Winners were displayed in the windows of Herpolsheimer's department store downtown for Queen Juliana's inspection.

Widening Our World View

The Museum continued to reflect and shape the attitudes of the community toward the world and our place in it. Christian Carron, a Public Museum Curator since 1988, believes that the development of ethnic exhibitions over the years has been driven by what is relevant to the community. "In the past, there was no National Geographic, no Internet, and less opportunity to travel and learn about the world," he explained in a 2003 interview. "The Museum did bring the world to Grand Rapids. People brought the world back with them. A good example: after World War II we opened Pacific Island Hall and Orient Hall—why did we suddenly have these things? Why did we care? After WWII suddenly we all knew where these places were." (More about the Museum's role in the patriotic life of the community can be found elsewhere in this book.)

In the late 1960s and early 1970s, Weldon D. Frankforter, who became Director of the Public Museum in 1965 (see Chapter Six), organized a series of temporary ethnic heritage displays, portions of which were re-installed as permanent exhibitions in Heritage Hall in the Museum's new East Building. Beginning with a celebration of French Christmas customs in

LEFT: The 1934 exhibition featuring the art and culture of the Netherlands, including hundreds of heirlooms and objects loaned by local residents, was the most popular event ever produced by the Museum and set the stage for an explosion of ethnic heritage projects. The exhibition ended with a pageant titled *Lovers of Liberty*.

BELOW: A Japanese Officer's Sword from World War II, donated to the Public Museum in 1954 by Richard Fleagle.

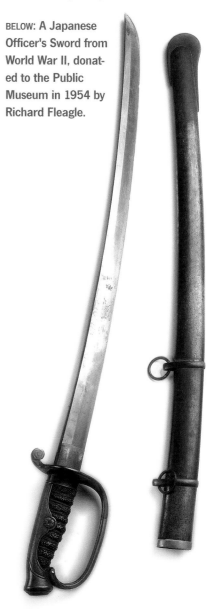

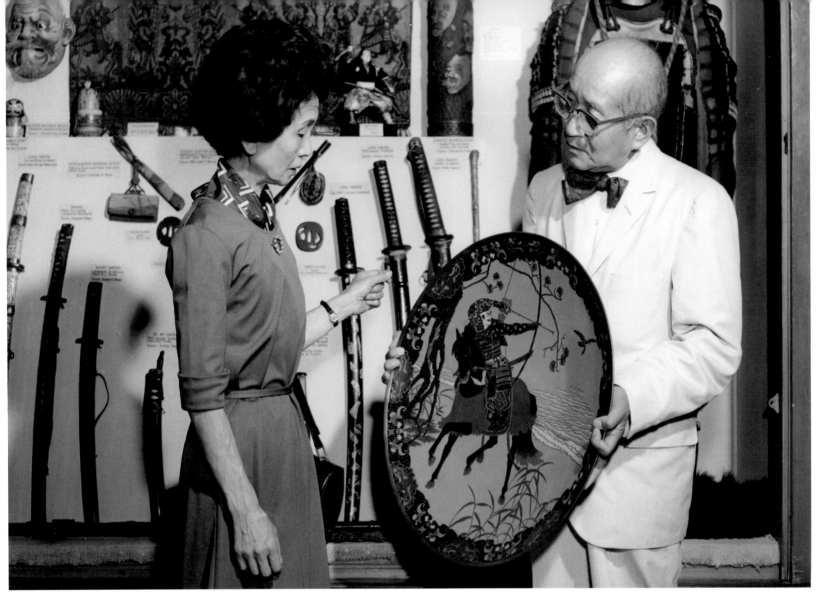

1967, and the dedication of a permanent exhibition case highlighting Polish heritage in March 1968, an extensive series of projects centered on *Grand Rapids Ethnic Heritage* was launched. In 1970 a *Dutch Heritage Exhibition* again brought the Ambassador from the Netherlands to the city, and in 1971, the Consulate General of the Polish People's Republic opened *Christmas Customs of Poland*.

The exhibition projects had effects far beyond Museum activities. In the Museum's 1972 Annual Report, Frankforter wrote, "As a result of our having initiated the Mexican Heritage exhibition a few years ago, the Latin-

Americans in our area have held an annual fiesta in the fall with parade, music, dancing and food." Frankforter had served as the Grand Marshal for that fall's Mexican Fiesta Parade. Community celebrations of Mexican-American heritage have continued to be a prominent feature of festivities in downtown Grand Rapids each fall.

Frankforter's plans for ethnic heritage programming were ambitious. In 1971, following the opening of the *Black American Heritage* exhibit, he wrote, "I look upon these displays as only an experiment or training ground for expanded exhibits which will be developed when more space becomes available. They are extremely condensed statements," he concluded. The

OPPOSITE TOP: Mrs. Oiwa Nabane, Japanese consul, and Mr. Kenji Nabane, from the Japanese Consulate in Chicago, visit the exhibition *Focus on Japan* at the Grand Rapids Public Museum in August, 1975.

OPPOSITE BOTTOM: Mr. and Mrs. Ralph J. Arriago and their daughter Theresa look at an exhibition honoring Mexican Independence Day, 1964.

LEFT: The Latvian Choir of Grand Rapids performs at a celebration in 1972.

BELOW: A parade from the Sheldon Complex to the Public Museum opened the African-American Heritage exhibition in September 1971.

Museum also continued its process of collaboration with local groups to develop the exhibitions. In 1987 a Citizens Committee formed to update the permanent African-American display.

Special temporary exhibitions and celebrations also were part of the Museum's ethnic programming. In August 1974, *Black History in Michigan* traced the roots of local African-Americans, and in 1975 *Focus on Japan* was part of a statewide International Week.

In December 1975, the American Association of State & Local History bestowed a special award of merit to the Public Museum for its ethnic heritage exhibits, the first time such exhibits had been recognized with that award. The projects had been profiled nationally in an article in *Museum News* in 1970, naming the Public Museum a model for ethnic programming, and in 1972, the American Association of Museums and the U.S. Department of Housing and Urban Development jointly published a case study of the

Museum's ethnic exhibitions and programs.

The Public Museum joined Grand Rapids Junior College and the Public Library in 1978 to form the Ethnic Heritage Consortium for a project funded by the U.S. Department of Education. Five local ethnic groups were studied, and materials were produced for teachers, for a series of cable television programs and for a mobile exhibit unit. The project included taped interviews and an accumulation of photography and data. The Heritagemobile was constructed, and was parked behind the East Building for school group visits.

In 1979, Museum staff set up three exhibit cases showing Indian beadwork of the Upper Great Lakes at the first (and since annual) *Homecoming of the Three Fires* Native

RIGHT: A Native American artist demonstrates soap carving during *Masters of the Arctic*, an exhibition of Inuit artwork that celebrated the kickoff of the campaign for a new Museum in 1989.

BELOW: Many treasured local family collections were donated to the Public Museum in 2004 in preparation for the ethnic history permanent exhibition at Van Andel Museum Center, including Polish heritage artifacts dating from ca. 1870 to the present from the collection of John J. Arsulowicz, Jr. Pictured is a first communion wreath and headpiece, ca. 1910.

American celebration, and in 1980 opened the major permanent exhibition *People of the Grand*, tracing the history of people in the Grand River Valley.

Frankforter's efforts to explore and celebrate the ethnic heritage of the region were, in his own evaluation, the highlight of his tenure as Director of the Public Museum. "I got acquainted with the most wonderful people in the community through those exhibitions," he remembered in a 2003 interview. "We were focusing on our own heritage—the point of view of a person coming to America, retaining their own culture. We gave the different groups the freedom to form their own committees and some really went on to do great things."

Other Museum staffers also mark the Ethnic Heritage exhibitions of that era as a milestone for the Public Museum. "*The Fabric of Jewish Life* exhibit in 1985 was probably the best temporary exhibit we had done to that point," said Marilyn Merdzinski, who joined the Museum staff in 1977 and became Registrar (now Collections Manager) in 1979. "The caliber of the story, the exhibitry, was just outstanding. We had to borrow pretty much everything—it was one of the largest temporary loan shows that we did. We borrowed something from nearly every Jewish family in town." Merdzinski particularly remembers a brass candlestick loaned by a local woman from her family's collection of Sabbath objects. "We were doing a condition report, which establishes the condition of an object when it is received," she explained in a 2003 interview. "It was very ordinary looking, but it turned out that this was the only thing her mother and father were able to smuggle out while fleeing from the Nazis. They left everything else behind. 'It's the only thing I have,' she told us, and here she was letting me take it and put it on exhibit. That is so powerful."

When the Public Museum moved from Jefferson Avenue to Van Andel Museum Center in 1994, a permanent exhibition about community diversity was part of the Exhibition Master Plan developed during the extensive planning

process for the new facility. Temporary exhibitions such as *Rainforest Adventure: The Gold, Jade & Forests of Costa Rica* in 1997, *Mysteries of Egypt* in 1999, and *The Dead Sea Scrolls* in 2003 continued to bring ideas and information about world cultures of the past and present to the city, but the goal of a major permanent exhibition about the ethnic cultures of Grand Rapids remained prominent. In 1996, an *Ethnic Heritage Celebration* raised funds to move the project forward and brought people of many nationalities together for a rousing series of music, dancing, feasting, and fun.

Community Planning, Community Culture

By the late 1990s, the Public Museum was embarking on an extensive research project and community dialogue that would frame the future ethnic history exhibition at Van Andel Museum Center. In the winter of 2001, Timothy J. Chester, Director of the Public Museum since 1988, announced that the process to make the exhibition a reality had begun.

Planning and research for the new exhibition involved two components. Major grants from the Institute of Museum & Library Services, a federal agency, and the National Endowment for the

Humanities (NEH) were awarded to help document the Museum's extensive collections related to world cultures. The process brought experts in the material culture of many ethnic groups to the Museum to examine the collections and provide crucial information about the objects.

Grants from NEH, and the local Frey and Grand Rapids Community Foundations helped to fund a second component of the process that is a familiar one for Museum staff and volunteers. "We want to once again engage interested members of our community in a spirited dialogue-and-research project," Chester explained in a 2001 interview in *Museum* magazine. "We have a long history of doing this."

A community advisory group was formed comprising representatives from the ethnic groups of the region, such as African-American, Jewish, Hispanic, Asian, Dutch, Polish, and German; members from fields of academic study including history, anthropology, sociology, and material culture; and others representing organizations striving for social change, such as the Woodrick Institute for the Study of Race and Ethnicity at Aquinas College and the planners of diversity curriculum for area schools.

From this group, which began meeting in the spring of 2002, the theme of the exhibition has been developed: the personal and family stories of actual people from West Michigan. The exhibition will be presented from the viewpoint of the people telling the stories, not from the Museum's. "The project is not planned as a homage to the 'old country,'" said Veronica Kandl, a member of the Public Museum staff since 1989 and exhi-

FAR LEFT: *The T.S. Dance Company* from Ottawa Hills High School, performing at the *Ethnic Heritage Celebration,* November 1996. From left, Chandala Walker, Kisha Gray, LeAssa Grady, Nikia Folden, Rufus Taylor, and choreographer Shannon L. Harris (also a Museum staff member). The Company was directed by Ernestine A. Harris.

LEFT: In 1978, as part of the local World Affairs Council's International Month, the Public Museum hosted an exhibition titled *The Art of the First Australians.* The following year, the Australian government, which had organized the exhibition, donated 25 pieces of Australian Aboriginal art and artifacts from the traveling show to the Public Museum, which were then installed in the Museum's South Pacific Hall. Many of the objects were seen again in 2002 at Van Andel Museum Center as part of an exhibition titled *Tjukurrpa: Australian Aboriginal Art of the Dreaming,* organized jointly with Grand Valley State University. Pictured here is a wooden ceremonial female figure carved by Sugarbag Katipi of the Tiwi aboriginal people of Melville Island, Northern Territory, Australia.

BOTTOM LEFT: The invitation for the opening of the exhibition *Rainforest Adventure: The Gold, Jade & Forests of Costa Rica* in 1997. The Gallery Guide was available in Spanish and English language versions.

ABOVE: **Members of a community advisory group organized for discussion and research for the new ethnic history exhibition at Van Andel Museum Center. From left, meeting in 2002, Patrick Rogan, exhibition designer from Threshold Studio, Public Museum Curator Christian G. Carron, Public Museum Director Timothy J. Chester, and Dr. David Pilgrim, Curator of the Jim Crow Museum of Racist Memorabilia at Ferris State University.**

bition curator implementing the vision of the group. "It's about getting here, being in Grand Rapids. How did people get here, why, when and where did they live, what their family was and is like."

Changing ideas towards race and ethnicity permeate the culture of 21st-century America. In an article for the March 2001 Museum newsletter *Discoveries*, Timothy Chester wrote, "few topics surface as regularly in our local news media as those which touch on issues of race or ethnicity." He described visits by members of the ethnic history exhibition team to the recently opened Lower East Side Tenement

Museum in New York City and the Jim Crow Museum of Racist Memorabilia at Ferris State University in Big Rapids, Michigan, and the assistance of curators at those institutions in planning the exhibition for VAMC.

In the Winter 2002 issue of *Wilson Quarterly*, Miriam R. Levin, a member of the Department of History at Case Western Reserve University, wrote, "In recent decades, a new generation of curators has sought to take account of new scholarship on class, race, ethnicity, and gender in the exhibitions they mounted. They have questioned both the progressive claims of Western science and scientists' assertions of

A modest artifact can tell an important story. The fishing boat bell pictured here accompanied a group of Vietnamese refugees on their flight aboard a small, overcrowded craft across the South China Sea, eventually landing in Pulau Besar Refugee Camp in Malaysia. In gratitude for their safe passage, the group hung the bell in the tower of a church. In 1979, the Reverend Howard Schippers, founder with his wife Marybelle of the Freedom Flight Refugee Center in Grand Rapids, was visiting the region as the camp was being disbanded. He was given the bell, and took it home to hang in the Center, where it was rung every time a sponsor was found for a refugee. It was donated to the Public Museum for the ethnic history exhibition at Van Andel Museum Center by Rev. Schippers, along with the Freedom Flight Center sign, painted in the colors of the Vietnamese flag by a group of refugees. The two objects now help to tell the story of the Vietnamese in Grand Rapids.

objectivity. The system of identification that had been used to categorize artifacts and organize history exhibitions on a continuum of progress was broken."

The new ethnic history exhibition at Van Andel Museum Center will represent the best efforts of the Public Museum to continue the story of Grand Rapidians as citizens of the world. Curator of Collections Christian G.

Carron believes that the new exhibition will reflect how our community has been shaped by the world. "At the time the old Heritage Hall was constructed, the displays were very cutting edge and won national awards for community involvement," he explained. "But the things that were provided and the story told was about the folk culture of, for example, Poland, or the arts and crafts tradition of Mexico. Today, we're talking about how those traditions have affected the community of Grand Rapids—what was brought with, what continues to be observed, how they affect the community at large still. It's the cultures of the world but in context of who we are here and now."

LEFT: Special events each weekend in October 1996 highlighted the cultural riches of West Michigan, celebrating 30 years of collaboration between the Museum and the city's ethnic communities and saluting Glea and W.D. Frankforter for their efforts in that collaboration. A steering committee helped to organize the programs, culminating in an *Ethnic Heritage Celebration* featuring food and entertainment from communities including African American, Chinese, Dominican Republic, Dutch, English, Filipino, German, Greek, Indian, Italian, Jewish, Latvian, Lebanese, Mexican, Native American, Polish, Spanish, Swedish, Thai, Vietnamese, and more.

Poster design by Ruth Oldenburg.

4. A New Museum 1932–1960

The Great Depression. Just the words conjure brooding black-and-white images of bread lines and soup kitchens, desperate dance marathons, dust bowl refugees and hordes of unemployed men riding the rails across America.

When the boom of the Roaring '20s crashed in 1929, the global economy steeply declined, until by 1932 one out of every four American workers was unemployed and the total value of world trade had fallen by more than half.

But for some American leaders, the calamity of the Great Depression turned into opportunity for progress and reform, for the American 'can-do' spirit to shine through at its best. From U.S. President Franklin D. Roosevelt to Grand Rapids City Manager and Mayor George Welsh to Museum Director Frank DuMond, the response to hard times would be: work harder.

Doing More with Less

Frank DuMond had shown that he could stretch the Kent Scientific Museum's meager funds to the maximum. An old automobile garage building southeast of the Museum at the corner of State Street and Waverly Place had been rented in 1932 to replace a former 'Museum Annex'

across Jefferson Avenue. As part of the drastic cutbacks that year that resulted in DuMond's appointment as Acting Director, the main building, the old Howlett mansion on Jefferson, had been shuttered and all Museum activities run from the State Street garage.

DuMond rose to the challenge, transforming the auto showroom into a popular public space and continuing an ambitious schedule of educational activities for schoolchildren. In 1933 the City Commission recognized his efforts by voting to increase the Museum's appropriation, praising it as one of the few agencies offering free 12-month entertainment and education to city residents. He responded with the record-breaking *Exposition of Dutch Arts & Crafts* in 1934 (covered in the previous chapter of this book) and other popular programs, including the first *Pioneer Days*.

In 1935, however, the lease on the State Street 'Annex' expired, and to save its $2400 annual rent, the Museum was forced to move back into its main building. The gloomy, cluttered old residence seemed even more inadequate to Museum staff, now numbering only four. But the seed of inspiration had been

ABOVE: Scrip issued in the early 1930s by the City of Grand Rapids to pay for public works programs during the Great Depression, including painting and carpentry projects at Kent Scientific Museum. From the collection of the Public Museum of Grand Rapids.

OPPOSITE: Frank DuMond with a book published by the American Association of Museums in 1950, prominently featuring the new Grand Rapids Public Museum that at the beginning of the Depression was little more than a dream.

planted in the fertile mind of Frank DuMond. "Our success in drawing record-breaking crowds into the State Street garage has taught us that accessibility is important," he wrote. "If Grand Rapids should ever find enough money with which to build a new museum I suggest it be brought out to the sidewalk line at street level and be windowless except for a few openings to attract the attention of passersby."

A New Deal

Franklin Delano Roosevelt was elected President of the United States in 1932 on a platform of recovery and reform. When he took office, most of the nation's banks were closed, more than 13 million workers were out of a job, and farmers were in dire straits. Within his first hundred days his administration had launched the most extensive peacetime legislation program in U.S. history, The New Deal.

In Grand Rapids, City Manager George Welsh was ahead of Roosevelt. When he was appointed in 1929, he embarked on an austerity program to turn the city's million-dollar deficit into a surplus. As furniture factories began closing following the crash, and unemployment ballooned, he was ready with a program of public projects and scrip labor that put thousands to work in 1931-32, culminating with the construction of the Civic Auditorium. Opened in 1933, it was renamed Welsh Auditorium in 1975 in recognition of the man who embodied the city's motto—*Motu Viget* (strength through activity). Forced by critics of his programs to leave office, Welsh was elected Mayor in 1938 in time to leverage federal public works funds into the city's first pipeline to Lake Michigan.

Frank DuMond was eager to take advantage of the flow

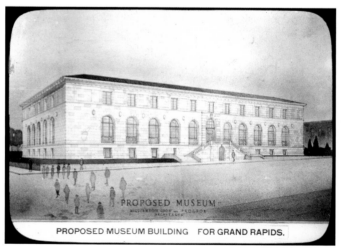

PROPOSED MUSEUM BUILDING   FOR GRAND RAPIDS.

of cash coming from Washington, D.C. In 1933, funds for "Museum improvement construction" were among 15 projects submitted by the City Engineer to qualify for federal public works money. There was a hitch, however. In order to receive government assistance for a building project, a matching "sponsor's fund" was required.

The city had asked voters for a bond issue in 1923 for an ambitious Municipal Museum that included an art gallery and historical furniture exhibits. The measure was soundly defeated, despite a booming economy. It was not likely the public would approve an appropriation, even to match the carrot of federal funds (one newspaper letter writer objected to the Annex lease in 1932 with succinct advice: "dump the junk in Lake Michigan ... rather than become an added burden to the taxpayers.") The question remained: where would money to match the federal funds come from?

Devising a Miracle

In Frank DuMond's unpublished *Narrative History of the Grand Rapids Public Museum*, he unambiguously titles the section about how WPA funding for a new museum building was secured, "A Miracle Happens." Closer to reality is that determined city staff and museum supporters devised a way to turn funds that had been problematic into the seed money for a WPA building grant.

In 1918, Estelle Provin died and bequeathed her considerable estate to the city of Grand

On the card: Provin, Mrs. L.S — DONOR — ACCESSION NO. 19___ — GIFT NO. 1591 — DESCRIPTION OF ARTICLE — CAT. NO.

LEFT: The City Commission's decision to use the Provin bequest for the Public Museum was not without controversy, as several other groups stepped forward to assert their claim to the funds. There is some evidence that Estelle Provin would have approved of the Commission's decision, however. In the collection of the Public Museum is a group of more than a dozen objects donated by Mrs. L.S. Provin during her lifetime, part of what is described in the 1910 annual report as an "interesting collection of botanical, mineralogical and ethnological specimens collected while on her travels." Although little survives of a botanical or mineralogical nature, hats, jewelry, baskets, domestic implements and other artifacts from South America attest to Mrs. Provin's interest in the Public Museum.

Card files used during the first years of the 20th century serve as both reference and artifact in the Public Museum's new Community Archives & Research Center.

OPPOSITE FAR LEFT: A lantern slide of the building design proposed to voters in 1923 to house a Municipal Museum, Art Gallery and Historical Furniture Exhibit.

OPPOSITE INSET: Identification badges were ordered by Frank DuMond in 1937 to reinforce the change of the institution's name from Kent Scientific Museum to Grand Rapids Public Museum.

Rapids for the founding of "a practical civic agricultural college," a communal farm for "persons or families who may have proven or be otherwise incapable of independence and self-support." Of course, no provision in the city's charter would permit such an undertaking, and Mrs. Provin had further encumbered her gift with a number of bequests and annuities that must be paid before the remainder of the estate could go to the city.

Mrs. Provin had been a teacher at the old Union High School and married Levi Provin in 1876. A devoted couple, they ran his real estate business together until his death in 1906, when she took charge and remained active in local business for the rest of her life.

After years of wrangling about the bequest, the city finally settled with the heirs. The City Commission had voted in June, 1936 to change the name of the Kent Scientific Museum, often mistaken for a county institution, to the Grand Rapids Public Museum, and in December they confirmed their responsibility to the municipal department by voting to allocate the entire amount of the Provin Fund to a new museum building project. At the ceremonies marking the laying of the cornerstone for the new building on April 9, 1938, Miss Clara M. Wheeler, a long-time friend of the Provins, remembered them as "civic-minded and forward-looking in aspiration … (with) high ideals of the value of education."

The Grand Rapids Plan

While the city prepared its application for federal funding, and the disposition of the Provin Estate was settled, the Museum Building Committee proceeded with an invitation to local architects to submit proposals for a new museum. Three firms prepared plans based largely on the ideas of Frank DuMond. Roger Allen, a member of the American Institute of Architects and President of the West Michigan Society of Architects, was chosen, in part for his knowledge of WPA-financed projects.

The design, which came to be known widely as the Grand Rapids Plan, was for an essentially windowless two-story structure of reinforced concrete, with a street-level entrance brought right up to the sidewalk line and five display windows set in walls facing Jefferson and Washington.

Although DuMond credited the Museum's three years occupying an old automobile showroom as inspiration for the open, welcoming design, it was an era of changing attitudes toward architecture and its role in public life. While the roots of modernism may be traced to the sociological and technological changes of the Industrial Revolution, it was the mid-20th century before many American architects began to reject the nostalgia of classical forms and embrace the machine age.

In 1932, the Museum of Modern Art in New York organized and toured an exhibition of models and photographs by avant-garde European architects, curated by Henry Russell Hitchcock and Philip Johnson, who introduced the term "International Style" to describe a new approach to building design. In a book about American museums to commemorate the 100th anniversary of the American Association of Museums in 2006, Marjorie Schwarzer, chair of the Museum Studies Department at John F. Kennedy University in California, writes that, "To modern architects, the Beaux Arts was more or less bunk. They summarily rejected applied historical ornament and symmetrical planning. Instead they favored a fresh style that focused on a building's function and exploited the qualities of industrial materials and technological advances. Concrete, steel, and plate glass were not only more economical than marble and stone, they were more of their times and thus more beautiful."

Frank DuMond was not the first to apply these ideas to museums. In 1926, John Cotton Dana, director of the Newark Museum in New Jersey, commissioned Chicago architect Jarvis Hunt, who had also completed a Macy's Department Store in Newark, to design what became one of the first modern museum buildings in the country. But, writes Schwarzer, "Dana was far ahead of his time. Nostalgic visions of a glorious past would reign in most of the nation for at least the next two decades."

Closer to home, however, ideas about modern design were percolating. In 1930, New York industrial designer Gilbert Rohde convinced D.J. DePree, the president of West Michigan furniture maker Herman Miller, of the virtues of modernism, launching a revolution that would result in work by some of the most significant designers of the 20th century. In 1937, architect Frank Lloyd Wright commissioned the Metal Office Furniture Company of Grand Rapids, forerunner to Steelcase, to manufacture

ABOVE: **Among the innovations in the new Public Museum building design that came to be known in museum circles as "The Grand Rapids Plan" were recessed display cases built into the walls of the Museum galleries. In a 1964** *Grand Rapids Press* **article, retiring Museum Director Frank DuMond reminisced about the design process for the Depression-era project. "We had (architect) Roger Allen design the display cases right into the walls," he remembered. "We knew we wouldn't have a nickel to buy display cases ... we'd have to move right in." Curator of Exhibitions Ardath Allen is pictured above with young visitor.**

RIGHT: **A desk and chair designed by Frank Lloyd Wright for S.C. Johnson & Son, manufactured by The Metal Office Furniture Co., forerunner to Steelcase, Inc. From the collection of the Public**

his radically modern furniture for the office building he designed for S.C. Johnson & Son in Wisconsin. Eventually, ideas crafted in West Michigan about office space and office furniture design would change the way people work all over the world.

Museum Launched on New Era

Records Are Perpetuated in Museum Cornerstone

CORNERSTONE RITES COVER PAST, FUTURE

Ceremony Called Realization of City's Fondest Dream for Education

PURPOSE OF BUILDING IS RECALLED BY MAYOR

By CARLETON CADY

Getting On With It

On October 11, 1937, President Franklin Roosevelt approved a grant of $103,175 in WPA funds for a museum building project to which the city of Grand Rapids would contribute $77,000. The following day, DuMond closed the doors of the red brick mansion that had housed the museum for 33 years, and a crew of WPA workers began dismantling the exhibits, which were trucked across town and stored in an unoccupied school.

By November the site had been excavated and on April 19, 1938, the cornerstone was dedicated with a civic ceremony. Construction proceeded until the summer, when it became evident that the estimates for the project had been too low. On August 27, 1938, the project came to a halt.

Roosevelt's New Deal programs were facing political opposition and new WPA rules strictly limited the use of its funds only to labor, and demanded heavy local contributions. In a letter to Mayor George Welsh, district WPA Director

A.D. MacRae wrote that the project had been discontinued pending provision by the city of further materials for use in construction.

More than a year passed, with fingers pointing and sarcasm issuing forth from city newspapers ("perhaps some day somebody will build a Museum to house the heap of stone and concrete which a long time past was supposed to have become the new Grand Rapids Museum," huffed the *Grand Rapids Herald*). Finally, the City Commission found additional funds, partly from liquidated assets realized from the Provin Estate, the architect and building committee modifed the plan, and construction resumed in October of 1939.

On January 9, 1940, the Museum staff, which had dwindled to just three, along with 17 WPA art workers, moved into the new building and began installing exhibits. The City's final audit of the project reported the cost of the structure as $208,901: $97,308 in WPA funds and $111,593 from City and Provin Estate funds.

"It's as friendly as were the late John Ball and Charles W. Garfield, pioneers, lovers of children and donors of local parks which bear their name and it's as accessible as your corner store," conceded the *Herald* on June 12, 1940, Dedication Day, though the newspaper had been severely critical of both the design of the

LEFT: **Although** *Grand Rapids Herald* **head-lines were optimistic at the laying of the cornerstone on April 19, 1938, it wasn't long before civic pride turned to sarcasm (ABOVE), in the summer of 1939 when construction was delayed.**

BELOW: **Architect's rendering of the front elevation of the new Grand Rapids Public Museum at 54 Jefferson SE.**

museum and the delay in its construction. "That's the beautiful new Grand Rapids Public Museum which will be dedicated to the residents of this city today ... as modern as today, so designed as to win unanimous approval of experts from points near and far."

The *Grand Rapids Press*, which had been more supportive, wrote that "The handsome new institution, a thing far apart from the dingy, grim and uncomfortable corridors which in the past have marked our own and other public museums, signalizes a new trend in the direction of stimulating study and search for knowl-edge among all age groups. Like the corner gro-cer who spreads his freshest strawberries and vegetables to tempt the public, the museum now brings its displays out of foreboding dark cor-ners and stalls and places them where they can be seen to advantage under proper lighting and in attractive arrangements."

The new museum began to draw national attention. A full-page article in *The Christian Science Monitor* on December 23, 1941 featured photos of the new Museum and its exhibitions (as well as two of DuMond's four children), and quoted DuMond's dream of "a new type

Education

A Tuesday and Saturday Page

A Museum 'as Accessible As A Dime Store,' as Friendly As a Next-Door Neighbor

By Karla V. Parker

Special to The Christian Science Monitor

Grand Rapids, Mich.

Scorning to hide behind the dignified term of "public relations," Frank L. Du Mond, director of the Grand Rapids Public Museum, says "The museum director is a salesman purveying a specialized type of goods. He will do well to study sales methods, advertising techniques, and commercial house displays, and adopt them to his needs."

How earnestly he believes in these precepts is indicated by the structure and planning of the Grand Rapids Public Museum which counts its visitors by hundred thousands. How contagious his enthusiasm is shown by the fact that he was able to convey to the Museum Commission and the City Commission his dream of a new type museum which would "be as accessible as a dime store," planned to "retail museum services to the public."

the general public that the museum was a major educational and recreational factor in community life.

It probably was these special exhibits that saved the museum. It certainly had its influence when a bequest fell to the city for a prescribed form of educational use. Mr. Du Mond's foresight, the support of the public now thoroughly interested in museum possibilities, the inability of the city to carry out the terms of the will, the cooperation of the heirs, and eventually the City Commission, resulted in a WPA project; and after a long wait, Grand Rapids had its new Public Museum.

Public Interest Continues

Public interest has continued with the completion of the building. For example, insistent protests by a number of organizations prevented the issuance of a liquor license to a near-by recreation hall.

museum which would 'be as accessible as a dime store' planned to 'retail museum services to the public.'"

The article also praised DuMond's efforts in education, and in securing the maximum benefit from WPA funding for exhibition construction. The writer described a series of carved scale models as "remarkable for their intricate and skilled artisanship," concluding that the work "is of a type which would be difficult or impossible to obtain in any but a town with the background of old-world manual craftsmanship long a part of the furniture industry."

It was not without some merit that the city began to boast of possessing "America's Most Modern Museum." In July, 1944 Laurence Vail Coleman, Director of the American Association of Museums in Washington, D.C., visited the

Grand Rapids Public Museum as part of his research for a book on museums of America. He commented, according to DuMond's unpublished history, "Museum structures similar to the one here are bound to come after the war. And, as in Grand Rapids, they will be in the center of cities, where they belong, instead of out in the outskirts."

When the book, *Museum Buildings, Volume One, A Planning Study,* was published in 1950, the Grand Rapids Public Museum was prominently featured, listed by Coleman as among "the best museums of the final prewar decade—the modern decade—of construction."

Making the Most of the New Museum

DuMond moved quickly to take advantage of his dream museum. With more than a half-mile of exhibit space in its well-lit, recessed cases, a large central hall and exhibit rooms on two floors, he could finally make good on his promise of a museum "accessible as a dime store and friendly as your next door neighbor."

He instituted a number of outreach pro-

GRAND RAPIDS PUBLIC MUSEUM

ABOVE: **A booklet about the Museum was distributed to visitors by the Grand Rapids Convention Bureau.**

BELOW: **One of the most-loved features of the new Musuem was the whale hanging above the main entrance, with a mezzanine balcony for observing the creature and pitching pennies onto its tail.**

grams, including weekly radio programs on WLAV and WJEF and newspaper features on the "exhibit of the week," displayed in a special case at the front of the building. In a 1948 *Grand Rapids Herald* article noting his 25th anniversary with the Public Museum, he reiterated his belief that the Museum should be "an educational institution for the public, it ought to lure the man on the street inside and make him glad he came," he explained. With increased exhibition space had come increased donations to the Museum's collections. "It takes careful planning to know what we should keep and what we should discard, because we have to choose what will be

of historical value 50 years from now," he mused, "what will tell the story of our culture."

For the next several decades, the Public Museum would have ample opportunity to implement those goals. With the coming of World War II, a renewed interest in patriotism and the roots of America would spark some of the most cherished Museum traditions. DuMond's ideas about serving wide interests and bringing in as many people as possible from all walks of life would result in such projects as the Youth Talent Competition, and the formation of an active Museum Association of community volunteers.

In 1958, after several thwarted expansion efforts, the city of Grand Rapids acquired the Medical Arts Supply building on Washington Street just east of the Museum building, and renovation began that would result in many new Museum features, not least of which was the acquisition of the Furniture Museum, which would bring to the Public Museum the story of Grand Rapids' most prominent business.

These events and their impact on exhibitions and activities are very effective examples of one of the Museum's most important functions throughout its history, preserving and telling the stories of our lives, which is the theme of Chapter Five of this book.

4.1 Artists Help Shape Museum

The public works projects of the Great Depression had a cultural and social impact still evident across the United States. Buildings, parks, and environmental projects helped to shape a uniquely American landscape, and works of art in many media created not only employment for artists but a lasting legacy of American cultural heritage.

The local and federal works programs of the 1930s afforded Museum Director Frank DuMond many opportunities to tap into the talents of local artists. In 1931, George Welsh's scrip labor program provided workers for painting and carpentry projects at Kent Scientific Museum's main building, and in 1933 funds from the Civic Works Administration provided carpenters, a taxidermist, and a colorist for renovation and construction of exhibit cases. Subsequent federal programs including the Federal Employment Recovery Act (FERA), the Works Progress Administration (WPA), and the National Youth Administration (NYA) provided craftsmen, clerks, and laborers for a wide variety of projects at the Museum.

While acquiring art is not explicitly part of the Public Museum's mission or practice, many works that document or otherwise shed light on the region's cultural, social, and natural history have made their way into the Museum's collec-tions. Artists are also employed on the Museum's staff as designers and preparators (more about the artistry of exhibition design and changing techniques used by Museum staff over the years can be found in Chapter Eight of this book). But many artists from the community and beyond have played an important role at the Museum throughout its history. Their work is most apparent in exhibition paintings, creating ambience and background and enhancing the stories told by artifacts.

In 1925, Director Henry Ward and Preparator E.A. Hyer cleared a large swath in the Kent Scientific Museum to install five diorama exhibits depicting Michigan mammals. To paint backgrounds for the first two, Wolf and Bear, they hired well-known nature artist Robert Bruce Horsfall from Washington, D.C., art director for *Nature Magazine* and a researcher and artist for the Smithsonian Institution. He had created many of the backdrops for the Smithsonian's zoological and botanical divisions, and for institutions including the American Museum of Natural History in New York and the Peabody Museum at Yale University.

A Timber Wolf diorama created in 1925 was so lifelike, a photograph of it was mistaken for the real thing by the *Detroit Free Press*.

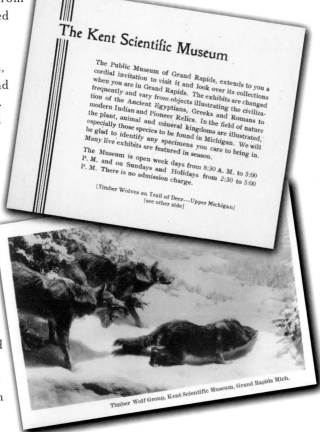

The Kent Scientific Museum

The Public Museum of Grand Rapids, extends to you a cordial invitation to visit it and look over its collections when you are in Grand Rapids. The exhibits are changed frequently and vary from objects illustrating the civilization of the Ancient Egyptians, Greeks and Romans to modern Indian and Pioneer Relics. In the field of nature the plant, animal and mineral kingdoms are illustrated, especially those species to be found in Michigan. We will be glad to identify any specimens you care to bring in. Many live exhibits are featured in season.

The Museum is open week days from 8:30 A. M. to 5:00 P. M. and on Sundays and Holidays from 2:30 to 5:00 P. M. There is no admission charge.

[Timber Wolves on Trail of Deer---Upper Michigan]
[see other side]

Timber Wolf Group, Kent Scientific Museum, Grand Rapids Mich.

A June 1936 article in the *Grand Rapids Herald* profiles "Negro artist Chase Pierce ... a merry, cultivated man, imaginative ... has been in residence in Grand Rapids a dozen years." The article also states that Pierce "is now painting the backgrounds for the historical dioramas being made as a WPA project under the direction of Frank DuMond, curator of the Kent Scientific museum."

BELOW: Intaglio prints by Reynold Weidenaar (1915-1985), including *Self Portrait* (TOP) and *Locomotive Shop* (BOTTOM) are in the permanent collection of the Public Museum.

The Timber Wolf exhibit became one of KSM's most popular, renowned for both its taxidermy and artistry, and photographs of it were widely circulated. On Sunday, September 2, 1928, The *Detroit Free Press* ran a four-column color halftone of a wolf group titled 'On the Hunger Trail,' under which they disclosed that the image, missing its explanatory material, was "pronounced a genuine photograph by the art department of this newspaper," probably the result of "a powerful telescopic lens." Of course, the photo was of the KSM exhibit, resulting in great glee at the local Museum. "It is a common occurrence at the museum for parents to experience much difficulty or fail entirely in trying to induce their young children to enter the room of our mammal groups, so fearsomely lifelike are they," wrote Director Ward in the local Press.

Many 21st-century visitors still feel a slight thrill when, rounding a corner in the Van Andel Museum Center's *Habitats* gallery, they are confronted by a restoration of the lifelike Timber Wolf group, now installed in its third Museum building.

Grand Rapids artists have also been important contributors to effective exhibitions at the Public Museum. Among the painters, woodcarvers, and exhibit builders Frank DuMond was able to hire with federal works funds were Chase Pierce, one of the city's first recognized African-American artists, and Jaro Hess, who has been called the most original artist of fantasy the city has produced. The two created dioramas for exhibits of Native American history and the life and times of Paul Bunyan. In 1940, WPA workers created a huge relief map of

Michigan, carved from wood, that can be seen at Van Andel Museum Center at the top of the south stairway.

Local artists also have been important as teachers in the Museum's education programs. In 1974, Joseph Kinnebrew, who went on to establish a national reputation, was an artist-in-residence at the Public Museum as part of a pilot program sponsored by the National Endowment for the Arts. His sculpture *Astronaut & Icarus* was donated to the Museum in 1985.

Reynold Weidenaar, one of the city's most celebrated artists, taught sketching classes at Blandford Nature Center in 1976. An archival collection of his graphic work, along with equipment from his studio, was donated to the Museum by Jay and Betty Van Andel in 1993. In 2003, Native American artists taught classes in basketry, beadwork and other skills in conjunction with *Tribes of the Buffalo: Karl Bodmer's Images of the American West, 1832-34*, which was an exhibition based on 19th-century works of art.

Paul Collins, another nationally known Grand Rapids artist, has created many works for the Museum, beginning in 1971 with murals of famous black Americans for the Museum's Heritage Hall. In 1975, he worked with the Museum's Native American Educational Committee on a presentation of his paintings of Sioux Indians. Proceeds from the exhibition and its publication, *Other Voices*, initiated a scholarship fund for Indian students. His 1980s work *Harriet Tubman's Underground Railroad* was donated to the Museum in 1996.

When the Museum moved to Van Andel Museum Center in 1994, many local artists were involved in construction of the exhibitions, including Ed Wong-Ligda, professor at Grand Valley State University, who painted the mural at the entrance to *The Furniture City*, and Jon McDonald, professor at Kendall College of Art & Design, who painted the cityscapes in *Streets of Old Grand Rapids*. Works by area artists also continue to be commissioned, including photographs of Michigan landscapes by David Lubbers in the permanent exhibition *Anishinabek: The People of This Place*, and paintings of the site of the village at Qumran in Israel by Stephen Duren in conjunction with the 2003 exhibition *The Dead Sea Scrolls*.

ABOVE: **A mural was created by Grand Rapids artist Ed Wong-Ligda for the entrance to** *The Furniture City* **permanent exhibition at Van Andel Museum Center in 1994. Pictured here is a cartoon made in preparation for the final product.**

LEFT: **Grand Rapids artist Jon McDonald creates a mural of the intersection of Monroe and Pearl for the permanent exhibition** *Streets of Old Grand Rapids* **in Van Andel Museum Center.**

5. Preserving and Telling the Stories of Our Lives

What is the Public Museum of Grand Rapids? It's full of rare and beautiful objects, but it's not an art museum. It abounds with flora and fauna from near and far, but it's not a zoo, or a botanical garden. It's a place for education, but not a school. The site of scholarly research, but not a library. A repository for a profusion of objects from the past, but not a warehouse, or an attic.

When a community advisory group came together in the early 1990s to plan the permanent exhibition at Van Andel Museum Center that would highlight the Native American history of the region, they were adamant that one feature absolutely must be included along with the Museum's treasured artifacts: the personal stories of the people, past and present. A similar advisory group working on the permanent exhibition that will highlight the diverse ethnicity of the region at VAMC came to the same conclusion: understanding complex issues comes from the real-life stories of individuals and families.

The people of West Michigan turn to the Public Museum for many stories of our lives. From a priceless Tiffany vase to a humble Vietnamese bell; from the beloved skeleton of a not uncommon whale to a handful of passenger pigeon eggs that are among only 129 still thought to exist in the world—each object has a remarkable story to tell, a story that can be told only by the real thing—a genuine, non-digital, right-there-in-front-of-you object.

In the years that followed the opening of the new Public Museum on Jefferson Avenue in 1940, Director Frank DuMond and his staff found new ways to relate the vast and growing Museum collections to community life, and in

BELOW: *Collecting A to Z* exhibitions at the Museum Center, such as *D is for Dolls*, include hundreds of treasures with stories to tell. Many significant dolls have been given over the years. More than 240 dolls from an impressive collection assembled by Mrs. Ben West (Antoinette Wurzburg West) were donated to the Museum in 1952 by her daughter, Mrs. John T. Osier, and family.

ABOVE: A cannon salvaged from an 1898 battle during the Spanish-American War and donated to the Museum in 1901 sat on the lawn of the old Kent Scientific Museum. In 1942, during WWII, the Kent County Defense Council sent a letter to the Board of Art & Museum Commissioners requesting its donation as scrap and "considerable publicity value" for the Salvage for Victory Clean-Up. The cannon was melted down for the war effort.

BELOW: The cannon's identification plaque was removed and remains in the Museum's collection.

doing so continued to tell stories that had deeply affected the people of the area for nearly a century, and are still being told to this day.

Several events in the two decades following 1940 set the stage for a discussion of these stories as they are told throughout the Museum's 150-year history: World War II brought a new attention to patriotism and the roots of American life and culture; the post-war baby boom and an affluent society with more leisure time widened the areas of interest the museum could serve; and the acquisition of another building, as well as the collection of another museum, dramatically increased the scope of exhibition—and story—possibilities at the Public Museum.

Patriotism and the Roots of America

December 7, 1941—it's a date that not only "lives in infamy," as President Franklin D. Roosevelt predicted in his speech following the bombing of Pearl Harbor, marking the U.S. entry into World War II. It was a date that changed how museums across the country would relate to their communities for decades.

Not two weeks after the attack, relates Marjorie Schwarzer in her book on the history of the American Association of Museums, a group of museum directors met in New York and issued a resolution: "If, in time of peace, our museums and art galleries are important to the community, in time of war they are doubly valuable. Museums must fortify the spirit on which Victory depends."

Back in Grand Rapids, Public Museum leaders were quick to rise to the challenge. In the Museum's annual report for 1942 (and reprinted in Grand Rapids newspapers), Emerson Bliss, President of the City's Board of Art & Museum Commissioners, wrote, "We are in this war not for material gain, but for the survival of the American Way of Life. We cannot close up, for the duration, the institutions we are fighting to preserve."

Only a few months after the U.S. entered the war, drastic cuts in City and school budgets resulted in Public Museum funding slashed by more than half. The WPA workers who had added so much to Museum enterprises were moved to Department of Defense activities. The entire staff except the Director and a janitor was laid off, and in November, 1942, Museum hours were limited to four afternoons a week.

Following the end of the war, the Museum created a War Relics Hall to contain many objects that had been collected from a variety of conflicts. Exhibitions continued to reflect a patriotic tone, such as Freedom Week in 1948, and a Freedom in Action Open House in 1952, co-sponsored by the Chamber of Commerce and highlighting "the American system of business and democracy."

World War II was not the only time that the Museum rose to a patriotic occasion to rally the community. In the early 20th century, Kent Scientific Museum issued its first call for "war relics," some of which, including significant Civil War treasures, can be seen today in the *V is*

for Veterans exhibition at Van Andel Museum Center.

Kent Scientific Museum's participation in a national project in 1917 to showcase nations allied with America in the Great War (World War I) is detailed in Chapter Three of this book, and that same year the Museum created an exhibit for the West Michigan State Fair that included weapons and military accoutrements "appropriate to the sentiment of our times."

Understanding Americanism

One immediate result of the patriotic fervor awakened by WWII was a renewed interest in the roots of America. The Public Museum had for many years collected hundreds of objects related to the earliest settlements in the Grand River valley and beyond. Frank DuMond had created a special exhibition hall on the second floor of the Kent Scientific Museum's garage annex in 1932 dedicated to pioneer history and relics, and in 1950, he pulled the artifacts together

ABOVE: Since Van Andel Museum Center opened in 1994, patriotic celebrations of the 4th of July and exhibitions honoring the men and women who have fought for their country continue to be an important part of Museum activities. On Memorial Day, 2000, the Museum opened *V is for Veterans,* dedicated to area men and women who served the U.S. armed forces from the Civil War to the present day. The exhibition features photographs and objects donated to the Museum, telling many stories of courage and commitment. It also incorporates contemporary photographs of veterans by David DeJonge with oral histories by Karin Orr created for a temporary exhibition titled *Michigan Veterans of Five Wars* featured at VAMC in 1998.

BELOW: At the end of the 19th century, a plan was developed to replicate the Liberty Bell for the World's Columbian Exposition of 1893. Materials of historical significance were collected, such as a sliver of the desk used by Thomas Jefferson while drafting the Declaration of Independence, and wood from the tree under which Generals Grant and Pemberton sat at the surrender of Vicksburg during the Civil War (the star in the detail inset is made from that wood). The materials proved unsuitable for casting a bell. The Daughters of the American Revolution joined the project, and it was decided instead to follow the biblical injunction to beat swords into plowshares. John Deere & Company of Illinois was commissioned to make a Peace Plow using more than 22,000 wood and metal relics. The plow was exhibited at the Exposition in Chicago, along with an elaborate guide booklet detailing the source of each material. It came to the museum in Grand Rapids from the family of George S. Knapp, who was in charge of the national tour of the plow.

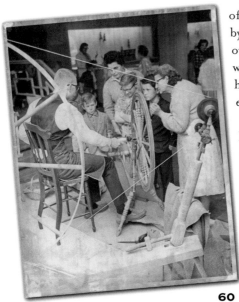

ABOVE: **Museum staffers Milda Purins, right, and Jean Keresztisi, work on a diorama of the cabinetmaking shop of William 'Deacon' Haldane, who came to Grand Rapids in 1836 and was thought to be the first person trained in furniture-making to ply his trade in the city.**

BELOW: **Learning to spin at Pioneer Days.**

INSET RIGHT: **A shirt made for the 1976 U.S. Bicentennial, celebrating Grand Rapids' own U.S. President Gerald R. Ford.**

again for a comprehensive permanent installation in the new Public Museum called *American Pioneer Hall.*

The project drew national attention, including a column in the *New York Sun* in which journalist Charles Messer Stow wrote that the exhibition "...tells the authentic story of Michigan's pioneer life in all its phases. Schoolchildren, many of them offspring of foreign-born citizens, here find a visual lesson in the kind of life typical of the early middle west. This leads automatically to understanding what is meant by the term Americanism."

The Museum had been hosting celebrations of pioneer heritage since the early 1930s, but by the late 1960s, the annual events stretched over five days. In 1972 a *Pioneer Harvest Festival* was initiated at Blandford Nature Center and has continued to be one of its best-attended events.

Gordon Olson, who was Assistant Director of the Museum from 1973 to 1979, when he became City Historian of Grand Rapids, remembers Pioneer Days as a "crazy, noisy, harried" time. "There was a steady stream of kids, bus after bus after busload," he reminisced in a 2003 interview. "Now, though, I think what an

incredible moment that was. What I was seeing was the passing of that generation. The 70- and 80-year-old people who were demonstrating were showing us skills that were passing with them, with the people of that generation." He explained that the visitors who were seeing the demonstrations at that time were seeing the real thing. "The people demonstrating then were showing things they learned as children—patiently explaining to one kid after another things like butter churning. I remember how kind and unflagging they were—as if they knew they had one last chance to pass this on."

In 1975, more than 16,000 people attended *Pioneer Days,* an enthusiasm attributed to the Bicentennial of the United States. The Public Museum was active in the celebration of the country's 200th anniversary, hosting meetings at Voigt House of the local celebration's Executive Committee, which included Museum Director W.D. Frankforter. Among the exhibitions and projects the Public Museum organized in conjunction with the celebration were re-publication of an historic atlas, the acquisition and restoration of the 1836 Calkins Law Office, which was dedicated on July 4, 1976, and placement of a time capsule inside a training capsule from NASA's Apollo moon exploration program in downtown Grand Rapids, now located in front of Van Andel Museum Center and slated to be re-opened in 2076.

The Museum's collection of early American artifacts is still among its most beloved. In early 2004, when interviewed for this book, Larry Shay, President of the Board of Art & Museum Commissioners, was asked to name his favorite object in the collection. "It's the George Washington memorial ring," he said without hesitation. "It's interesting partly just because we have it. That's an odd thing—it's not at

Mt. Vernon, or in the Smithsonian. It's intriguing to me that we have such an object, because you know there's some story about people that caused us to have it. I love the fact that we have it. When I'm with a group that doesn't know much about the institution, I drag it out for shock value. It speaks to what objects really are—they fulfill a primary instinct for storytelling, and that object really does it for me."

"Accessible as a Dime Store and Friendly as Your Next Door Neighbor"

Frank DuMond's description of the new Museum building in 1940 was not only a characterization, but could also be thought of as a mission statement. He set out to make the museum a meeting place for the community, a place for entertainment as well as education, and an institution that would serve the widest variety of interests.

The Director enlisted the help of local radio stations, producing programs such as *Nature Adventures*, *Nature Spy* (with Mary Jane Dockeray) and *Grand River Adventures*, and later a weekly television series, *This Amazing World*. A weekly newspaper feature was inaugurated in the *Grand Rapids Herald*, a relationship that also resulted in one of the Museum's longest-running and most successful projects, the *Youth Talent Exhibit*.

The idea germinated at a Midwest meeting of newspaper promotion men, attended by *The Herald's* publisher, who were confronted by a group of high school students complaining that young people were often portrayed negatively. Upon his return, Publisher Louis A. Weil, Jr. encouraged his staff to come up with a project to generate favorable publicity for area youth.

The result, after consultation with Frank DuMond, was the *Youth Talent Exhibit*, a joint ven-

LEFT: One of six memorial portrait rings ordered by Martha Washington as gifts for each of the bearers at the funeral of President George Washington in 1799. One of the rings was brought to Ann Arbor in the early 1800s, where it was bought in 1880 by the mother of Mrs. David R. Church of Grand Rapids. She sold it to the Public Museum in 1956. Created by the French artist Charles St. Memin, the ring is made of gold, with an inset copperplate engraving of Washington covered with glass. Thomas Jefferson is said to have described the ring as "the best likeness of Washington I have ever seen." Other surviving rings are in the collections of the Metropolitan Museum of Art in New York and the Smithsonian Institution's National Museum of American History.

From mementos of past presidents to relics left by the pioneers of West Michigan, the Museum's collections are rich with artifacts that speak of history and the roots of America.

Rix Robinson was a representative of the Hudson Bay Trading Company and ran trading posts east of Grand Rapids. In the 1820s, he ordered an elaborate safe (RIGHT) from New York, which found its way into the Public Museum's collections in 1917. The surface of the safe conceals a system of knobs that must be turned to reveal the key hole.

When James A. Garfield was elected the 20th president of the United States, he reportedly had trouble finding a top hat (he wore a size 7⅞). One of his former students at Hiram College, a man named L.W. Heath, was a hat maker and promised him a perfect fit. Heath presented the President with a silk top hat (BELOW LEFT) on inauguration day, March 4, 1881. Garfield was wearing it just four months later when he walked into the Baltimore and Potomac Railway Station in Washington, D.C. and was shot by a disappointed office seeker, Charles J. Guiteau. He died on September 19. One of the guards picked up the hat and gave it to Mrs. Garfield, who later returned it to the maker. It was given to the Public Museum in 1946 by Mrs. Frederick K. Tinkham of Grand Rapids, a daughter of L.W. Heath.

Millstones (RIGHT) were originally sent by the U.S. government to Native Americans for an operation north of Grand Rapids early in the 19th century. They were acquired by John Ball in the mid-19th century and served as a horseblock at his home for many years. The stones were presented to the Kent Scientific Institute in 1904 by his daughters, and rested outside the Kent Scientific Museum, then next to the Grand Rapids Public Museum on Washington Street. In 1994 they were moved to a spot alongside the Grand River, just below Van Andel Museum Center.

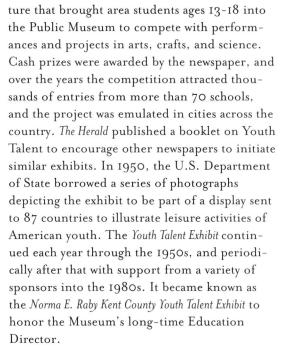

ABOVE: Frank DuMond, right, Public Museum Director, with Richard Yonkers, Director of the Grand Rapids Art Gallery, discussing the *Youth Talent Exhibit* in 1948. Local children showcased their skills in crafts such as woodcarving (TOP RIGHT), also in 1948, and inventive projects such as a hand-made snowmobile (BOTTOM RIGHT).

ture that brought area students ages 13-18 into the Public Museum to compete with performances and projects in arts, crafts, and science. Cash prizes were awarded by the newspaper, and over the years the competition attracted thousands of entries from more than 70 schools, and the project was emulated in cities across the country. *The Herald* published a booklet on Youth Talent to encourage other newspapers to initiate similar exhibits. In 1950, the U.S. Department of State borrowed a series of photographs depicting the exhibit to be part of a display sent to 87 countries to illustrate leisure activities of American youth. The *Youth Talent Exhibit* continued each year through the 1950s, and periodically after that with support from a variety of sponsors into the 1980s. It became known as the *Norma E. Raby Kent County Youth Talent Exhibit* to honor the Museum's long-time Education Director.

In 1952, a group of community leaders came together and formed the Grand Rapids Museum Association. At the first meeting on March 28, trustees were elected and by-laws enacted for an organization "to supplement and expand the services of the Grand Rapid Public Museum to the benefit of the entire community." As previously covered in Chapter Two of this book, the Museum Association, later known as the Friends of the Public Museum and now the PMGR Friends Foundation, became a primary partner with the Museum in many educational and fundraising activities, exhibitions, events, and publications.

In 1954, the new Museum Association was key to organizing events to celebrate the Museum's Centennial, including a parade on October 30 and an open house on November

28 that brought nearly 3000 to the Public Museum to sample a huge birthday cake. The centenary concluded on April 27, 1955 with a pageant at Civic Auditorium titled *A Century of Music in America.*

Many community organizations have found a congenial welcome at the Public Museum, and several held their first meetings there, including the Grand Rapids chapter of the World Affairs Council in 1953, the Grand Rapids Amateur Astronomical Association (co-founded by Museum Education Director Evelyn Grebel) in 1955, the West Michigan Environmental Action Council in 1968, and the Natural Areas Conservancy of West Michigan in 1976. The Museum hosted the first Michigan Historic Preservation Conference in 1970, and organizational meetings for the city's celebration of the U.S. Bicentennial in 1976 were held at Voigt House.

The Kent Garden Club moved its headquarters into the Museum from 1942-1945 from its home at the Grand Rapids Furniture Museum, and permanently when the Furniture Museum was moved to the Public Museum. It remained a part of the Museum until the late 1970s, becoming in 1952 the Grace Spears Chadwick Memorial Garden Center in honor of its long-time director.

The Grand River Folk Arts Society held concerts and dances at the Public Museum from 1978-2002, and countless local clubs and organizations have held exhibitions, demonstrations, sales, and other activities at the Museum, including the Grand Rapids Rock & Mineral Society, the West Michigan Quilters Guild, Boy Scouts and Girl Scouts, and many more. In 2000, Van Andel Museum Center was the site of one of the primary community forums in the City's Master Plan process.

The Public Museum also serves an important role as a center for social education and interaction. Working with a number of community organizations, the Museum has presented exhibitions and programs that explore complex and difficult topics, such as *Field to Factory: Afro-American Migration 1915-1940, Altered States: Alcohol and Other Drugs in America,* and *The Nazi Olympics-Berlin 1936,* the first major traveling exhibition organized by the U.S. Holocaust Memorial Museum in Washington, D.C., which made its national debut at Van Andel Museum Center in 1997. In 2003, *The Dead Sea Scrolls* brought nearly a quarter-million visitors to the Museum for a deep and significantly relevant experience of the common religious heritage of Jews, Muslims and Christians.

Not all the stories the Public Museum has to

FAR LEFT: The Museum's celebration of its 100th birthday ended on April 27, 1955 with an event in Civic Auditorium featuring over 400 performers and attended by more than 3000. Following a script written by *Grand Rapids Press* music critic Gerald Elliott, the pageant featured the Grand Rapids Symphony, Schubert Club, St. Cecilia Chorus, Great Lakes Barbershop Chorus, True Light Baptist Church Choir, a Dixieland band, and many more ensembles, as well as actors, dancers, and other performers. A 28-minute audio tape was made of selected portions of the program and broadcast nationally over the Mutual Broadcasting Company's 800-station radio network in May.

LEFT AND BELOW: The Public Museum has worked with many community organizations to present exhibitions that explore complex and difficult topics, including the Grand Rapids Alumnae Chapter of Delta Sigma Theta Sorority, Inc. for *Field to Factory: Afro-American Migration 1915-1940,* in 1991, and Project Rehab and other social service agencies for a 1997 exhibition titled *Altered States: Alcohol and Other Drugs in America.*

tell are completely serious and weighty. Many unconventional and entertaining moments can be found in its education and exhibition history. *Meet the A-Bomb*, an exhibit from the American Museum of Atomic Energy at Oak Ridge, Tennessee visited the Public Museum for ten days in January, 1955, not an especially light-hearted topic, but followed in February by a symposium on flying saucers attended by more than 1000 people. In 1986, the Chaffee

plotting to expand the facility. One grand scheme included an aquarium and a roof garden, and in 1947 a committee of war veterans and Gold Star mothers proposed a museum addition as a World War II memorial. The question was put to the voters, however, and the idea for a $750,000 Museum War Memorial was defeated in a controversial election in which only property owners could vote.

Museum supporters did not give up. The newly formed Museum Association approached the City Commission with a plan for a $450,000 addition as part of the Centennial Year Celebration in 1954, but was turned down. As a token to recognize the 100th anniversary, the Commission voted to appropriate $25,000 for a Museum Building Fund, a commitment they continued in budgets over the next few years.

In 1957, the Grand Rapids Furniture Museum Commission, which had been established in 1938 to oversee a collection and exhibitions in a 19th-century Tudor mansion on East Fulton Street, resigned, citing diminishing attendance and declining participation by manufacturers who had helped create the museum. They recommended that the collection be turned over to the Public Museum, and the mansion be sold to finance exhibition space at the Jefferson Avenue building.

ABOVE: Although many visitors were thrilled by the Klingon wedding at Van Andel Museum Center, many more learned the actual science stories behind the speculative fiction of *Star Trek* in a 2001 exhibition.

RIGHT: The Planetarium's show about the return of Halley's Comet set a new attendance record in 1986, and its Comet Pills generated interest nationally, with publicity on *The Today Show* and the *ABC Nightly News* and in *Time* magazine, earning the Museum's staff a Public Relations Society of West Michigan award for the idea.

Planetarium organized a series of *Comet Watches* and other activities to greet the return of Halley's Comet. A popular item at the event was the Museum's own Comet Pills. And Museum audiences had their own opportunity to go where no one has gone before with *Star Trek: Federation Science* at Van Andel Museum Center in 2001.

The Stories of Business in the Furniture City

When the new Public Museum building opened in 1940, Frank DuMond and the Board of Art & Museum Commissioners were already

At about the same time, spurred by increasing interest in space exploration, a group of local foundations, corporations, and interested individuals were contributing to a fund to build a planetarium at the Public Museum. In an article for the Winter 1961 *Midwest Museums Quarterly*, Frank DuMond wrote "The jigsaw picture puzzle situation in which we were becoming involved still lacked the most important component," namely, a building plan that would accommodate the proposed features, at a cost less than the figure previously denied.

In the article, DuMond recounts his

moment of inspiration: "A member of our Museum board came into my office to talk ... about our proposed addition with its estimated $450,000 for 30,000 square feet of floor space. There wasn't a chance the City Commission would find the money for it. As I gazed out of the window across the Museum's backyard, I seemed to see for the first time the big two-story automobile showroom, garage and service building next door ... Why don't we buy that building?" (DuMond's inspiration may not have been quite so spontaneous as the demands of a good story imply. The Overland Automobile Company, which built the structure in 1917, offered it to the city in 1921 for $130,000 as a home for the Kent Scientific Museum. More recently, the Public Museum had been renting space in the building, which housed the Medical Arts Supply Company, for storage.)

The Board of Art & Museum Commis-

ABOVE: A display at the Grand Rapids Furniture Museum, which opened in 1938 in the former home of lumber baron T. Stewart White at 527 East Fulton. The project was initiated by the Chamber of Commerce, working with the local Furniture Manufacturers Association, with some funding from the WPA. It was promoted as a major Michigan attraction, the only museum in the country exclusively devoted to furniture. After the War, manufacturers began concentrating on market showrooms, and increasingly auto-borne tourists found its limited parking an inconvenience. The Furniture Museum closed its doors on February 15, 1959 and all exhibitions that had become the property of the City of Grand Rapids were moved to the Public Museum's newly acquired East Building on Washington Street. Many pieces from its collection eventually became part of *The Furniture City* exhibition at Van Andel Museum Center.

RIGHT: Museum Director Frank DuMond, right, mounted many cooperative projects with local businesses, such as an exhibit of toy banks at the People's Bank in 1948.

RIGHT: When the Phoenix Furniture Factory was pulled down in 1988, the Museum salvaged materials from the oldest parts of the building, which now can be seen in a permanent exhibition at Van Andel Museum Center showcasing the city's heritage as *The Furniture City*.

INSET BELOW RIGHT: A promotional booklet from 1904.

The most recent efforts to collect and study the history of the Grand Rapids furniture industry were begun in 1979 as part of the Museum's 125th birthday celebration, with the long-term goal of organizing and presenting a major permanent exhibition drawing on the institution's comprehensive collection of more than 2,000 examples of Grand Rapids-made furniture. In what Museum Director Timothy Chester described as "the mammoth process of its organization," it became clear that marshaling the volumes of artifacts and historical data in the collection could be the basis for a major publication. In 1998, the idea came to fruition with *Grand Rapids Furniture: The Story of America's Furniture City*, by Christian G. Carron with contributions from Kenneth L. Ames, Jeffrey D. Kleiman, and Joel Lefever. Since its publication the book has been widely recognized as the definitive work on the subject and a valued resource for scholars and collectors throughout the country.

sioners lost little time in proposing the 47,000 sq. ft. building to the City Commission. It was purchased for $319,000 and plans for converting it into exhibition space were put into motion. The acquisition set the Public Museum on a track of growth that would continue over the next two decades, detailed in the next chapter of this book.

The acquisition of the Furniture Museum provided the impetus for dramatic growth in another aspect of the Public Museum's service to the area, preserving important artifacts and communicating the business history (and stories) of the community.

Local businesses had long been partners with the Museum in showcasing the commercial activities of the city and region. In 1915 a Museum Development Association was organized to promote "exhibits from Industries advertised over the country," which, in the newspaper language of the day, demonstrated "the commercial advantages to be had from a modern museum." In 1932 the first of a series of temporary exhibits featuring Grand Rapids industries focused on the commerce that built the city, the lumbering industry.

The Furniture Museum collection made it possible for the Public Museum to become the premier environment for the story of Grand Rapids as the Furniture City, a story that continues to be central to the history and development of the region. In 1958, the Michigan Historical Commission acknowledged the importance of the enterprise by issuing Kent County's first Historical Marker, recognizing the Grand Rapids Furniture Industry. The Marker stood for many years on Washington Street outside the Public Museum, and was moved in 1998 to a place of honor next to Van Andel Museum Center.

In 1961, a Furniture Wing was opened in the East Building, exhibiting the treasures in stylized period rooms. The Museum continued to work with local businesses to showcase their products and stories, including an exhibit in 1981 sponsored by the Furniture Manufacturers Association titled *150 Years of Furniture History*. The Museum joined the Grand Rapids Art Museum and Kendall College of Design in 1985 to present the *Furniture City Expo*, and that same year published *Grand Rapids Made: A Brief History of the GR Furniture Industry*.

When the Museum was planning its move to a new facility on the Grand River downtown, ideas about exhibitions were changing. "The period rooms in the old Museum showed us recreations of how people lived," explained Curator Christian G. Carron in a 2003 interview. "When the Public Museum acquired Voigt

House (in 1974, covered in the next chapter of this book), there was the opportunity to show real use. But at Van Andel Museum Center we could really tell the story of how furniture was made and sold."

In the Exhibition Master Plan developed in 1989 during the planning process for the new Museum, consultant James E. Sims wrote that *The Furniture City* exhibition would explore how the social and cultural history of the region had been shaped by the furniture industry. "As we see the furniture industry change from makers of chairs to marketers of 'environments' we share a changing perception of the meaning of things. This is not only a narrative history of the city; it is a history of a change in consciousness. Our relationship to work and the products

ABOVE: *The Furniture City* exhibition at VAMC is an example of the way interpretation of collections is changing. Curator Christian Carron describes it as 'a 10,000 sq. ft. furniture exhibit that's not really about furniture at all—it's about the people who made the furniture, the people whose lives were affected and how they use it." When Carron was asked to name his favorite object in the Museum's collections, he had an unusual choice. Frank Davidhazy donated his furniture decorating studio from a nearly seven-decade career that began in 1922 to the Museum.

"Frank and his son, Frank Jr., served as our living community artifacts and links to the furniture industry when we were creating *The Furniture City*," explained Carron in a 2003 interview. "Frank Sr. had an incredible sense of history, and kept his tools and everything throughout his whole production. When we opened VAMC, Frank Sr. was wheeled in by Frank Jr. and the first thing he said was 'That's where my visor is! I've been looking for it.' He reached out with his cane to get it and Frank Jr. said 'no, that's the community's now.' That willingness to turn over a piece of his life—something he'd worn since the 1920s—it was extraordinary." The humble and worn visor (RIGHT) is Carron's pick of the collection.

ABOVE AND RIGHT: In 1991, Bissell Inc., Grand Rapids manufacturer of cleaning products marketed worldwide, donated its archives and comprehensive collection of more than 1000 carpet sweepers, dating from the mid-19th century, to the Public Museum. In 2002, the Museum created an exhibition titled *Grand Rapids Cleans Up: A History of Housekeeping* in honor of Bissell's 125th anniversary.

Since Van Andel Museum Center opened in 1994, the Museum has continued to tell the many stories of business and its impact on the life and history of the region. The Museum has collaborated with a number of businesses and organizations to create exhibitions commemorating significant milestones in their history, including the 150th anniversary of Blodgett Hospital, the 80th of the local chapter of the American Red Cross, and histories of Butterworth Hospital, WOOD-TV, the Grand Rapids Ballet, and others.

of our work is different. As a material culture study this exhibition asks 'What are things? How do they mean?'"

The Joy of Stuff

What are things? How do they mean? Stephen Weil, noted American writer and former official at the Smithsonian Institution, is quoted by Miriam R. Levin in an article titled "Museums and the Democratic Order" in *The Wilson Quarterly*, Winter 2002: "Discomforting as the notion may be to many of its advocates, the museum is essentially a neutral medium that can be used by anybody for anything …

Museums are at their best and most distinctly themselves when they deal with 'stuff,'" wrote Weil. Levin adds, "The process by which that 'stuff' is chosen, displayed, and interpreted is how these storehouses of detritus function as agents of social change."

Storehouses of detritus? Well. Another American writer, poet Donald Hall, published a collection of memoirs in 1960 that told small and seemingly inconsequential stories about his childhood summers with his grandparents in New England. His opening relates the story of a man cleaning the attic of an old house, who comes upon a box full of tiny pieces of string. On the lid of the box is written, "String too short to be saved." Like those tiny pieces of string, Hall's small stories, collected, were full of meaning and value.

Collecting, preserving, presenting—those are the action words of the Public Museum's mission, and have been applied equally over the last 150 years to an astounding variety of objects, mundane and sacred, that give meaning to the stories of our lives. From objects that have long disappeared, such as Buffalo Bill's camel, stuffed and turned over to the Kent Scientific Museum following its demise at John Ball Zoo in 1911, to treasured antiques and heirlooms of immeasurable value bestowed on the Museum by knowledgeable and passionate enthusiasts, the collection has grown to staggering proportions. "It's a collection that has been assembled from everyone in town," quipped Curator Christian Carron in 2003, "one donor at a time."

Decision-making about what to collect and what to reject has changed over the years. An active Collectors Club has been in existence since the late 1930s, and continues to meet regularly to share interests and knowledge. A number of the Museum's major collection donors have been members, and the Collectors Club has a tradition of supporting the Public Museum by funding acquisitions for it when asked, including, over the years, glass, lamps, pottery, rugs, needlework, clocks, and much more.

Until recently, however, decisions about

what to collect were largely staff-driven. In the fall of 2002, a board-appointed community group was organized to review every object, large and small, that is submitted to the Museum for acquisition. The Collections Committee reflects many constituencies, and is an example of how the Museum has become a very public, very community-based institution, according to Carron. "It's just not practical to save everything," he explained in a 2003 interview. "Just as we do with exhibitions and programs, we want the community to tell us what's relevant. As with all community groups, it would probably be easier for staff to do it by themselves—it always takes more time. It makes our jobs harder but it makes the product better."

"It's probably the most vital thing a museum can do," said Museum Director Timothy Chester at a February 2004 Collections Committee meeting. "It proves that the Public Museum is not just about old things from the past—it's connecting people, engaging them in the work of the museum, which is preserving things for a particular use. Once we've decided we can't collect everything in the whole wide world, we need to identify research needs and display needs, and consider sensitive matters of history and personal attachments. It's true community control of a community museum."

Collectors and collecting are among the Public Museum's most important connections with the community. The Grand Rapids Collectors Club has presented many important artifacts to the Museum since the 1930s, including (TOP) a rare 19th-century Japanese cabinet. Pictured here in 1953 are, left, Mabel Perkins, President of the Collectors Club, and Mrs. Sanford P. Wilcox, Secretary of the Museum Board of Directors.

In 1998, the Public Museum celebrated personal collecting on a grand scale with *Magnificent Obsessions*, an exhibition of 24 remarkable collections and profiles of the people who assembled them, culled from more than 175 submitted for consideration in a year-long process. CENTER: Rick Overway, with his amazing collection of toy robots.

Many large and valuable collections have been purchased for or bequeathed to the Public Museum over its 150-year history. They have been used in a variety of exhibitions, and most recently can be seen throughout Van Andel Museum Center as part of the *Collecting A to Z* exhibition that showcases the Museum's permanent collection. In 1938 the estate of Lansing collector Susan Stebbins Stark donated nearly 500 valuable antiques and more than 100 reference books to the Museum, including a collection of 50 antique cast-iron penny banks (BOTTOM) that have continued to delight both young and old savers in *N is for Numismatics*.

6. Growth and More Growth 1960—1976

The purchase in 1958 of the former automobile showroom on Washington Street just east of the WPA-era Museum building more than doubled the size of the Grand Rapids Public Museum, and launched two decades of exceptional growth for the institution.

It was also an era of dramatic, and painful, growth for the U.S., with aspirations as high as the moon and dreams of equality and justice resulting in turmoil, tragedy, and lasting social change. The race to modernize the country was accompanied by a soundtrack of destruction and disorder—and the stirring of voices defending historic and environmental treasures, as well as new voices demanding a place at decision-making tables.

Elephants & Leopards, Oh My!

Museum Director Frank DuMond, now nearing an age when most people would begin to think about rocking chairs and golf, forged ahead with ambitious plans for the new facility. Even before the Museum officially occupied the space, he was using it for his favorite events—public spectacles that drew hundreds of people.

"When we acquired the East Building, it was a mess," remembered Mary Jane Dockeray in a 2003 interview. "Dewey (Frank DuMond) was a Shriner and he loved the circus. When it came to Welsh Auditorium, he would use circus people on his radio and television programs. He made friends with the big cat trainer and when they had a layover, Dewey invited him—no committee meetings, no board approval—to bring

OPPOSITE: **The Apollo 1 astronauts, from left, Roger B. Chaffee, Edward H. White II, and Virgil I. (Gus) Grissom.**

BELOW: **School children entering the East Building, ca. 1962.**

his cats to the East Building." Dockeray, who was working in the Museum's Education Department (prior to her years as Curator of Blandford Nature Center), went along with the plan. "We sent out 'emergency bulletins' to the schools: 'Come and See Wild Cats Trained!' I can't believe we did that!" she exclaimed. "Even before that, Dewey made friends with the elephant trainer and hatched a plan to walk the elephant from Civic Auditorium to the Public Museum to interview the Mastodon! Think of the liability! When it got there we started to think—uh oh. But that was Frank DuMond."

Despite his unflagging energy, DuMond was far-

sighted in seeking out a kindred spirit to take on the challenges and opportunities of the vast new space. In 1962, Weldon D. Frankforter, Director of the Sanford Museum and Planetarium in Cherokee, Iowa, was named to the new post of Assistant Director of the Grand Rapids Public Museum. "Frank was a lot like Dewey," said Dockeray, "an opportunist. That's what you really needed to be in the museum field."

A geologist and paleontologist by training, Frankforter was an instructor in the geology department at the University of Nebraska, where he received his undergraduate and graduate degrees. He became Director of the Sanford Museum in 1951, and quickly assumed leadership roles with the Midwest

72 The Presence of the Past

Museums Conference, the Iowa Archaeological Society, and the Iowa Society for the Preservation of Historic Landmarks, affinities he would bring to West Michigan along with his energetic wife, Glea, and their five children. He was named Director of the Grand Rapids Public Museum in 1965.

The new position of Assistant Director was approved by the City Commission in 1962, according to Alfred W. Hewitt, President of the Board of Art & Museum Commissioners, to assume the added responsibility of operating the East Building, as well as a new planetarium.

The Space Age Going Lickety-Split

The idea of a planetarium had been planted in the minds of Museum supporters at the first meeting of the Grand Rapids Museum Association, a group that later became the Friends of the Public Museum, then the PMGR Friends Foundation in 2003. The first planetarium machine demonstration in the city was held as part of the meeting in March 1952 to organize the Association, and it wasn't long before community enthusiasts began a campaign to install a planetarium at the Public Museum in its own wing.

More than $65,000 was raised from private sources, and just as the first human being, Yuri Gagarin, was being launched into space in April 1961 by the Soviet Union, Grand Rapids audiences were being launched on their own star journey. In an article about the new Grand Rapids planetarium in the *Detroit Free Press*, a visiting professor was quoted urging citizens to visit the new facility. "With the Space Age going lickety-split," warned Henry Krul, a lecturer at the Hayden Planetarium in New York and native of Grand Rapids, "it's time for everybody to sharpen up on such things."

There were a few glitches with the new machinery, and the enterprise had

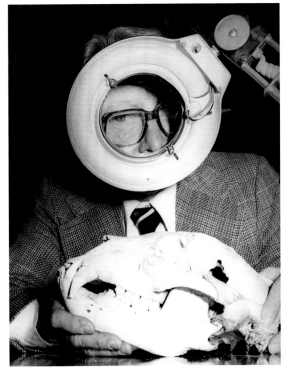

its share of stops and starts, but by 1963, the Museum was ready to hire a full-time curator to make the most of the new technology.

David L. DeBruyn was home in Muskegon for summer break from graduate studies in astronomy at the University of Michigan. "I heard a rumor that they needed a planetarium lecturer and I came snooping around," he said in a 2004 interview. Although DeBruyn was still in school, W.D. Frankforter spotted the potential in the young astronomer. "We hit it off well—liked each other from the start," said

OPPOSITE TOP: A circus elephant is introduced to the Public Museum's Mastodon skeleton at the main building, 54 Jefferson SE, in 1951.

OPPOSITE BOTTOM AND LEFT: "I had not the vaguest idea of going into the museum business," reminisced W.D. Frankforter in a 2003 interview. "When I was a kid the people across the street from us got the National Geographic, and I was on their doorstep the day it arrived. They said, 'Have you thought about geology?'" He enrolled at the University of Nebraska, where "Geology was in the same hall as the Museum Lab, and they were paying 25 cents an hour for students to prepare fossils." he explained. "Then I got a summer job digging things up. I had thought I was going to be an oil geologist and make a lot of money, but I was so fascinated with this, I thought I'd rather have an interesting life than one that's profitable. So I got involved with the museum—I evolved from the study of rocks to the museum business."

BOTTOM: Planetarium equipment from Spitz Laboratories was demonstrated at the organizational meeting of the Grand Rapids Museum Association, March 28, 1952. Despite a concerted effort, the only person who could be reliably identified in the photograph at left, taken at that meeting, is Mrs. Frances Baldwin, second from right, the aunt of Dr. Ralph Baldwin, first president of the Museum Association and a key figure in securing a planetarium at the Public Museum.

ABOVE: Planetarium Curator David L. DeBruyn in 1966, appreciating the clarity of an instrument from the Goto Optical Company of Tokyo, purchased in 1962 after difficulties were experienced with the first planetarium equipment.

RIGHT: Don & Blanche Chaffee, Roger B. Chaffee's parents, at the May 1967 dedication of the Roger B. Chaffee Planetarium with Gene Cernan, who, with Jack Schmitt, spent more than three days on the moon in December 1972, the last and longest U.S. lunar mission.

DeBruyn. "It was a wonderful opportunity." DeBruyn started on January 1, 1964, and went on to enjoy one of the longest careers in the Museum's history, still actively serving as Curator Emeritus in 2004. "Who could ask for a better job," he declared. "I'm a lucky person who found what he wanted to do and have done it for 40 years."

A milestone for the new Museum Planetarium came in January 1967, when a flash fire on the launch pad at Cape Kennedy, Florida, killed the crew of the Apollo space capsule during a simulation of their scheduled February launch. Grand Rapids native Roger B. Chaffee, along with Virgil I. (Gus) Grissom and Edward H. White II, became the first casualties of the U.S. space program. The Board of Art & Museum Commissioners voted to name the Museum Planetarium in honor of the young astronaut, and the Roger B. Chaffee Planetarium was dedicated on May 19, 1967. One of the guests at the dedication, remembered David DeBruyn, was Gene Cernan, who would be the last person to walk on the moon as part of Apollo 17 in 1972.

Less than a year after DeBruyn

became Curator of Astronomy, he was asked to start a weekly column for The *Grand Rapids Press*. In 2003, Press Editor Mike Lloyd wrote a tribute to *West Michigan Skies* as the longest-running column in the local newspaper. DeBruyn cites the column as one of the particularly rewarding aspects of his career with the Planetarium, and as another the establishment of Veen Observatory.

In 1955, Evelyn Grebel, the Museum's long-time education coordinator, and James C. Veen, a local astronomer who was killed only three years later in an automobile accident, co-founded the Grand Rapids Amateur Astronomical Association (GRAAA). The nascent organization held its first meeting at the Grand Rapids Public Museum, beginning an association that has continued nearly 50 years. The group realized their dream in 1970 when, after five years of weekend and evening volunteer work by astronomers-turned-builders, they opened the James C. Veen Observatory near Lowell, fifteen miles east of the city. The Museum continues to assist financially, and Chaffee Planetarium staff help the GRAAA run the Observatory, which has expanded and improved greatly over the years.

From the time of its opening in 1961, to its move to Van Andel Museum Center in 1994, the Museum's Planetarium hosted more than a million visitors for sky shows on topics ranging from the historic first moon landing in 1969 and Halley's Comet in 1985-86, to shows created specifically to accompany exhibitions such as *Dinomania*. In 1988 the Planetarium acquired a multicolored laser projection system that enabled the production of creative light shows set to music by recording artists such as Pink Floyd and Radiohead that draw large enthusiastic audiences.

The biggest decision in

the Planetarium's history, however, was the departure from the basic technology of moving lights and gears that, said DeBruyn, "hadn't changed much since it was developed in 1925." When a new Planetarium was being planned for a new Public Museum on the Grand River downtown, it was decided to take the leap into the new technology of computer simulation. "I was not totally in favor of it at the time," remembered DeBruyn, "but am really glad we did. The original planetarium was a geocentric look at the sky from the earth—it gave us a pristine sky image and beautiful reproduction." The new technology, based on the concept of Digistar developed by Evans & Sutherland of Salt Lake City, was a computer-generated projection with a fish-eye lens and a cathode ray tube. "This revolutionized the whole planetarium business," explained

DeBruyn. "Not only could you simulate the night sky, you could travel into that sky—have space experiences."

And space experiences are exactly what DeBruyn and his staff, including dozens of young high school and college interns who have gone on to significant careers in science and astronomy, have provided in the new 145-seat facility on the second floor of Van Andel Museum Center. The Digistar technology, a mega-watt sound system, and the capacity for a number of surprising special effects, such as realistic rain showers, have kept the Chaffee Planetarium one of the Public Museum's most popular attractions, as well as a significant resource for multi-media education. Among the accomplishments that DeBruyn points to with pride are shows created totally by the local Planetarium team, including *Age of*

ABOVE: The whale skeleton was a prominent feature of the Museum building that opened in 1940. It hung from the ceiling of the main hall until 1974, when, controversially, it was removed and put in storage. The bones of the skeleton and the structure that supported it were deteriorating, but Museum Director W.D. Frankforter promised that the whale would be reassembled at a later date, "hopefully, well within ten years."

Fourteen years later, just as Frankforter was moving into retirement, the whale was resurrected to become the focal point of a campaign to raise money for a better storage facility for the Museum's collections. With funding support from Fred Meijer, Meijer, Inc., and Steelcase, Inc. the whale skeleton was shipped to Chicago for conservation and new hanging armature. It was installed at Woodland Mall as the centerpiece of fundraising events and an exhibition of Museum treasures there in late 1987, and was returned to storage until the new Van Andel Museum Center was opened in 1994.

RIGHT: The whale skeleton over the Galleria in the Van Andel Museum Center. One of the first tasks for Museum staff after the beloved beast resumed a place of honor above the new Museum Center's Galleria was to finally track down just what the skeleton represented. The Museum's Assistant Director, Kay Zuris, and Curator of Natural History, Scott Rawlins, consulted with Dr. James Mead, Curator of Marine Biology at the Smithsonian Institution's National Museum of Natural History. He flew to Grand Rapids in August 1994 to examine the specimen, and concluded that it was not a blue whale, as long believed, but a finback whale, a member of the same family, *Balaenopteridea*. He also said that the skeleton was one of the most complete he had ever seen exhibited in a museum, and that the living whale would have measured 70-75 feet long and weighed in at 80-90 tons.

Discovery: Perugino and the Rebirth of Science and Exploration in fall 1997, which was the Museum's contribution to a city-wide celebration of art and culture titled *Grand Renaissance*, and *The Dead Sea Comes Alive* in 2003, what DeBruyn calls "the highlight of my career," produced to accompany the blockbuster exhibition *The Dead Sea Scrolls*.

Feet on the Ground

While the outer reaches of space seem to hold infinite fascination for the modern age, the mysteries and pleasures of the planet Earth have always exerted a fundamental appeal as the basis for understanding ourselves and our place in the universe.

From the very beginning of the Museum's history, collecting and interpreting the natural world has been one of its principal objectives. From John Ball and his comrades in the Grand Rapids Lyceum of Natural History, to the nature-hiking boys of the Grand Rapids Scientific Club, to Emma Cole's extensive botanical research, the early days of the Public Museum were dedicated to documenting and understanding the marvelous variety and inter-connectedness of life.

One of the chief objects of wonder in the Museum's early days was a large whale skeleton acquired in 1909 from the estate of Dr. Jacob W. Velie, of St. Joseph, Michigan, who was a commissioner of the World's Columbian Exposition in Chicago in 1893. The Kent Scientific Institute exhibited the leviathan at the West Michigan Fair to raise funds for a special whale barn behind the home that housed the Museum on Jefferson Avenue to exhibit it (a photograph of the early whale barn can be found in Chapter One of this book).

By 1910 the Kent Scientific Institute was reporting nearly a quarter-million shells in its collection and more than 2500 birds eggs. In 1917 a significant group of three Passenger Pigeons, nest & eggs were installed in the Michigan Bird Room.

Frank DuMond, a forester by training, had

an interest in natural history well-documented in his newspaper columns and community activities. Paleontologist W.D. Frankforter extended Museum activities in a variety of expeditions, including archaeological and biological research ventures to the Aleutian Islands co-sponsored by the Museum in the early 1970s.

But it was Museum Nature Lecturer Mary Jane Dockeray who spearheaded what would become one of the city's most significant commitments to natural history and environmental awareness. Dockeray, who joined the Museum staff fresh out of Michigan State College, was a Grand Rapids native who grew up on Collindale Avenue on the west side of the city. She had worked in the Museum's summer program while still in college, and Director Frank DuMond advised her to add some Natural History courses to her Geology degree program, and he would try to find funding to add a full-time Nature Lecturer to his staff. "I was in that job from fall of 1949 to fall of 1968," Dr. Dockeray remembered in a 2003 interview. "I went to about four schools a day, took kids on field trips, went camping. At a recent Land Conservancy event, the acceptor of an award came up to me and said 'I am so excited to meet you again—you came to my school 40 years ago.' That's just thrilling to me." The award, incidentally, is named after Mary Jane Dockeray.

One of the places Miss Dockeray, as she was then known, led her field trips was to Collins Woods, a favorite playground of her youth. "The road ended at a gate and we'd walk down a path I had made," she recalled. "It's a different world now—imagine taking kids on field trips on private land!" One day she saw surveyor's stakes. Victor Blandford had purchased the land during the Depression and used it for family and scout troop outings. It turned out the stakes

Among the most poignant of the Museum's collected specimens is perhaps the modest Passenger Pigeon, a bird that was once extremely common throughout North America. In the early 19th century, great flocks were reported to block out the sun for extended periods of time. Pigeon hunting became a lucrative business, both for food and for feathers, and their habitat was disappearing under pressure from agricultural development. By 1870 their numbers began to diminish perceptibly, and after 1890 sightings of even single birds were rare. Some protective legislation was passed, but it was too late.

In a June 1922 *Grand Rapids Herald* article, Museum Director H. L. Ward recounted an effort by the National Audubon Society at the beginning of the 20th century to determine if any of the species still existed anywhere. After three years of maintaining a standing reward of $1000 for any information about the birds anywhere in North America, "not a single bit of creditable evidence, not even a feather, had been brought forth." The last known living Passenger Pigeon was born in captivity in the Cincinnati Zoo and died there in 1914. The Kent Scientific Museum "is fortunate in possessing a mounted group consisting of two males, a female and a nest with a single egg," wrote Ward. "One of the males was taken in (Kent) county June 7, 1879."

The Public Museum actually has several eggs in its extensive oological collection. Passenger Pigeon eggs were in the news again in 2003 when a collection in a small East Texas town's historical association revealed two eggs believed to be from the extinct species, adding to the 129 still thought to exist, according to experts quoted in a National Public Radio report on the find. Tucked away in the Public Museum's natural history galleries on the third floor of Van Andel Museum Center are two of the rare birds, one in the cabinets of wonder in the Kent Scientific Institute room and one representing the sad story of extinction in the *Collecting A to Z* exhibition *Z is for Zoology*.

By the time Dr. Dockeray retired in 1989, the Nature Center had grown to 143 acres. In 1966 the Museum Association launched a campaign to finance construction of an interpretive center, which was dedicated in October 1969, thanks also to labor and materials donated or provided at cost by members of the local Contractors & Suppliers Association. Designed by the Lansing architectural firm of Frank & Stein, the cedar and fieldstone building is a wonderful example of the mid-century modern aesthetic of bringing natural light into the interior and using materials harmonious with the structure's surroundings.

Over the next three decades, Blandford Nature Center would become the hub of a wide range of activities, from tapping maple trees in the Sugarbush to the construction of a Sugar House in 1981 to pancake suppers where thousands enjoyed the sweet treat of maple syrup; from field trips for legions of school children, scout troops, and family groups, to the establishment of the Blandford Environmental Education Program in 1974 (covered in Chapter Two of this book). With the aid of public and private grants, the Nature Center grew to include a Wildlife Care Facility in 1993, a barrier-free trail system, a Naturalist in the Classrooms Program, and much more.

In a flurry of building relocation, a Pioneer Heritage Complex also was established at Blandford, including the Robinson-Kuhtic Log Cabin, built in 1866 by William Tyler Robinson and

RIGHT: Victor Blandford, center, assists his grandchildren Betsey Spayde, 8, and Martha Blandford, 2, in breaking ground for the new nature center in January 1968.

were not part of development plans, but it wasn't long before Mary Jane Dockeray and Frank DuMond were sitting at his dining room table in North Park drinking cider, eating donuts and discussing the 10-acre parcel. "In the mid-1960s, people didn't know what a nature center was," Dockeray explained, "but I did know that pretty soon you wouldn't be able to wander around on private property to go into the woods."

Victor and Marion Blandford made the donation, and the Museum and the City worked over the years to acquire surrounding land.

donated to Blandford by the Kuhtic family in 1971; the Stilwill Horse-Shoer Shop, donated to the Museum in 1971 and moved to Blandford in 1982; Star School, built in 1853 at 8th Ave. & Lincoln in Talmadge Township, and Centennial Barn, built at Edison Centennial Farm on Lake Michigan Drive, both donated and moved to Blandford in 1975. The historic buildings are often open to the public with intepretors and demonstrators offering a glimpse of 19th-century life.

In 2004, the Public Museum entered an innovative partnership with the Grand Rapids Public Schools to lease the Nature Center to the school district, allowing the schools to expand environmental education to many more students from throughout the city, and meeting a budget challenge posed by decreases in city, state, and federal museum funding. "The Public Museum and the Grand Rapids Public Schools have enjoyed almost 150 years of working together for the benefit of the school children of Grand Rapids," wrote Museum Director Timothy Chester in the January 2004 newsletter *Discoveries*. "This lease opens a new chapter in that relationship." He added that the Museum's education department would refocus its environmental education programs in the natural history galleries and labs at Van Andel Museum Center, while taking programs out to schools, parks and nature centers, including Blandford.

Natural history programs have been an inte-gral part of the Public Museum's purpose since its earliest days. But in the 1970s, a profound shift was taking place from the idea of natural history primarily as a source of wonder and curiosity to an awareness of the educational mission of science to focus on the interconnectedness of life on earth. The establishment of Blandford Nature Center was part of the Museum's response to those needs, and programming at the Museum's exhibition facilities also reflected questions about the interdependence of individuals and communities.

When Van Andel Museum Center opened in 1994, significant natural history galleries were designed to take visitors through the Grand River valley to interactive exhibitions exploring the variety of ecosystems found in the region. Museum planners also chose the natural history galleries to illustrate changes in Museum exhibition ideas and techniques from the earliest cabinets of wonder at the Kent Scientific Museum, to the innovative exhibition dioramas at the 1940s Grand Rapids Public Museum, and leading into the new interactive open dioramas in the permanent exhibition *Habitats* at the Museum Center. In an article about the new galleries in the April 1993 issue of *Discoveries* newsletter, Museum Director Timothy Chester wrote, "Our objective is to show the relationship between cultural beliefs, attitudes and values and how nature was observed, studied and described. To do this we need look no further than the history of the museum itself!"

LEFT: The R.B. Stillwill Horse-Shoer Shop, constructed in 1869, was donated to the Public Museum and moved to a spot behind the Museum from Jamestown in 1970. It was moved to Blandford Nature Center in 1982.

BELOW: Butterflies collected in the earliest days of the Museum can still be seen in a replica of a room in the old Kent Scientific Museum at Van Andel Museum Center. More contemporary ideas about how nature is observed, studied, and described are evident in the interactive open dioramas in the permanent exhibition *Habitats*, bottom.

ABOVE: John R. Stiles, left, and Robert Honting inspect a portico from the Vernon Hotel on West Fulton Street. It was razed in 1959 to prepare for the U.S. 131 freeway. In the late 1950s and early '60s, more than a hundred buildings in downtown Grand Rapids and more than a thousand homes on the west side were razed as part of "urban renewal." Many were ground into rubble and dumped into Riverside Park as landfill. Thanks to the efforts of Public Museum staff and volunteers, many historic artifacts and architectural fragments were salvaged and preserved.

Although the city became more sensitive to historic preservation, the Museum still plays a role when battles are lost. In 1988, when the Phoenix Furniture factory was being pulled down, the Museum salvaged materials from the 1876 building. Remnants can be seen in *The Furniture City* exhibition in Van Andel Museum Center.

Activities and exhibitions continue to involve Museum visitors with ideas about the natural world. In 1996, *Yikes They're Back* returned marvelous robotic dinosaurs to the city, but also brought renowned paleontologist Jack Horner to Meijer Theater for a lecture about his remarkable discoveries in the mountains of Montana. (Horner was not the first famous scientist to share details about astounding discoveries with Museum audiences. In 1966, L.S.B. Leakey was the guest of the Museum Association and the Coffinberry Archeological Society, and five years later his son Richard Leakey gave a lecture about the revelations of their excavations in Kenya, co-sponsored by the Public Museum and Grand Valley State College.) An exhibition about insects titled *Backyard Monsters* set new attendance records at Van Andel Museum Center in 1997. Several of the *Collecting A to Z* exhibitions in the Museum Center showcase the Museum's vast natural history collections, including *F is for Fossils*, *R is for Rocks & Minerals*, *Y is for Yearlings*, and *Z is for Zoology*.

Motu Viget—Strength Through Activity

While people all over the world were awakening to the importance of preserving the natural world, a number of concerned citizens also were organizing to preserve the quickly diminishing wonders created by our ancestors. "Crowbars, sledges and pneumatic hammers are busy wrecking a good part of our city's heritage," wrote John R. Stiles, chairman of a group of Museum volunteers working to salvage historic artifacts in the wake of freeway and shopping mall progress. His 1959 letter to *The Grand Rapids Press* sought assistance in a rescue effort that would become part of one of the Museum's most distinctive permanent exhibition installations, *Gaslight Village*.

After the Public Museum purchased the East Building in 1958, the necessity of connecting it to the existing structure evolved into an idea for an indoor street of shops evoking the 'gaslight era' of old Grand Rapids. The giant historical diorama was the brainchild of Frank DuMond, who stayed on after his 1964 retirement to see it through. A fundraising committee led by L.V. Eberhard raised $150,000 for the construction, and *Gaslight Village* opened in May, 1967. "*Gaslight Village* was a real community effort," remembered Robert Bushewicz, Staff Artist and Chief Exhibit Preparator for the Museum from 1961-1980. "People kept bringing in things to donate—

LEFT: Grand Rapids grocer and Museum volunteer fundraiser L.V. Eberhard looks at renderings for *Gaslight Village* in 1962 with Laurence A. Johnson, of Syracuse, New York, author of *Three Centuries of Country Storekeeping in America.*

OPPOSITE BOTTOM: One of the most beloved objects in *Gaslight Village* was a horse-drawn streetcar donated to the Museum in 1948 and stored outside the building until construction of the exhibition. The streetcar was in use in the city in the late 19th century, and was donated to the Museum by Louis J. DeLamarter, President of the Grand Rapids Motor Coach Co., successor to the Grand Rapids Railway Co.

The street car was removed in 1992 and underwent extensive restoration before being reinstalled at Van Andel Museum Center, marking the entrance to the *Streets of Old Grand Rapids* permanent exhibition.

the whole basement was full before we even started on it. Ardath Allen (Museum Registrar and Curator of Exhibitions from 1952-1980) was doing two jobs and was working with us, so the stuff just kept piling up downstairs."

In 1971, the Museum was again the beneficiary of the preservation zeal of John R. (Jack)

Stiles, a local builder. Stiles and his wife Mary purchased the historic Calkins Law Office and donated it to the city. (Mary Stiles is perhaps best known as the woman who chained herself to a wrecking ball to publicize the ultimately unsuccessful efforts to save the 19th-century City Hall clock tower in 1969. Many artifacts from the Richardsonian style building, and its story, are preserved in *C is for City Hall* at Van Andel Museum Center.)

The small Greek Revival building was built in 1836 and was the office of attorney Charles P. Calkins, a Vermont native who came to the city at the same time as John Ball. In the late 1960s, it was identified as the city's oldest surviving structure, and a preservation effort was launched. Thanks to Stiles and the newly formed Kent County Council for Historic Preservation, with help from the Grand Rapids Bar Association, Museum Director W.D. Frankforter arranged for the building to be

BOTTOM LEFT: The Calkins Law Office, built in 1836, originally stood on the corner of Monroe & Justice (now Ottawa), and was moved in 1853, and perhaps more than once, ending up in an industrial area on Ionia NW. It was moved to State Street, next to the Public Museum, in December 1971, restored and furnished by the Museum with financial support from community organizations. The dedication of the building was part of the celebration of the city's Sesquicentennial and the U.S. Bicentennial on July 4, 1976, and a book about the building and the efforts to preserve it was published by the Museum Association. The building was opened to the public during special event days, and is currently preserved as an historic landmark structure at the gateway to Heritage Hill.

Among the treasures that became part of *Gaslight Village* and can be seen today in the *Streets of Old Grand Rapids* permanent exhibition at Van Andel Museum Center were the complete contents of the Lindberg Gun Shop and Rudell's Drugstore.

RIGHT: W.D. & Glea Frankforter welcome visitors in the Rudell Drugstore during a *Gaslight Village* Open House, 1981. The turn-of-the-century drugstore was donated by the children of William Rudell of Sault Ste. Marie in Michigan's upper peninsula in 1971. The family selected the Public Museum from a number of institutions interested in parts of the store, including the Smithsonian Institution and Disney Corporation, because they wanted it to remain in Michigan and be preserved intact as it was in 1900. Its solid cherry cabinets, shelves, and drawers were full of historic items—over 13,000 were cataloged by the Museum registrar.

LEFT: Museum Director Frank DuMond is inspecting a portable forge in 1958 with Miss Anna Lindberg and Mrs. Thomas Vidro, daughters of Charles Lindberg, and Henderickus Bruins Slot, who haunted the Lindberg Gun Shop as a boy and helped the Museum arrange it in *Gaslight Village*. Much of the equipment was originally brought to Grand Rapids shortly after the Civil War by Charles Lindberg (not of flying fame), and his sons continued to operate it until the 1950s.

OPPOSITE PAGE: Built in 1895-6 by Carl and Elizabeth Voigt, the home at 115 College SE is now a property of the Public Museum of Grand Rapids. It was designed by Grand Rapids architect W.C. Robinson, loosely based on a chateau in France.

moved to tiny Lincoln Place park at State and Washington Streets, right next to the Public Museum.

Queen of the Hill

By the mid-1960s, many concerned citizens in Grand Rapids, Kent County, and across the U.S. were beginning to realize that the post-war building boom and the doctrines of urban renewal were wreaking havoc on the fabric of American cities. In 1966, Congress passed the National Historic Preservation Act, setting standards and establishing mechanisms for a National Register of Historic Places. Locally, the fight to save Grand Rapids City Hall, though unsuccessful, energized the Kent County Council for Historic Preservation, as

well as groups of neighbors concerned about plans for areas near the already ravaged downtown. (In 1974, critic Robert Sherrill wrote in *The New York Times Magazine*, "Urban renewal went through Grand Rapids like a $50 million glacier ... the downtown area ... is as lifeless as the inside of the corner mailbox after the last pickup.")

Members of the Heritage Hill Association, organized in 1969, were determined that their neighborhood of architecturally significant and beautiful buildings would be saved. In 1971 the area was registered as a National Historic District, becoming the largest urban historic district in the country at that time.

Also in 1971, Ralph Voigt, the youngest son of 19th-century Grand Rapids businessman Carl Voigt and his wife Elizabeth, died in the family home on College Avenue SE in the heart of Heritage Hill, leaving the Victorian Chateauesque-style mansion and all its contents to the Grand Rapids Foundation. The German-American family were partners in the Voigt-Herpolsheimer & Co. dry goods store and later the Voigt Star and Crescent Flour Mills on the west bank of the Grand River, where, interestingly, Van Andel Museum Center was built more than a century later.

The Grand Rapids Foundation leased the home to the Kent County Council for Historic Preservation (KCCHP) in 1972 for operation as a living museum. Public Museum Director W.D. Frankforter was Vice President of KCCHP at the time, and also had been appointed one of two representatives from Michigan to the National Trust for Historic Preservation Board of Advisors. James Biddle, President of the National Trust, came to the city in conjunction with activities surrounding the establishment of Heritage Hill, and also visited the Public Museum and attended a reception at Voigt House.

In 1974 KCCHP purchased the property and donated it to the City of Grand Rapids. Voigt House continued to operate under a committee of the KCCHP, with oversight by the

City's Board of Art and Museum Commissioners. In 1989 responsibility for daily operations was transferred to the Public Museum of Grand Rapids, which maintains the home and its collections as a living museum.

"Voigt House is one of only a few house museums in the country to have all of its original furniture and family possessions still intact," said Christy Ham, site manager of Voigt House since 1987. "It offers a glimpse into the lifestyle and values of an immigrant family that realized the American dream at the turn of the century."

The opulent home, built in 1895-6, its gardens, and carriage house remain one of the city's outstanding landmarks. The collection includes nearly 100 years of family furnishings from rare treasures to mundane daily utensils. It provides, in addition to nostalgic beauty, "a field site to study how people used furniture," said Museum Curator Christian Carron in a 2003 interview, a place where, in Carron's words, used in a popular campaign for the house, "the sofas run free." The home is open for tours during regularly scheduled hours, and hosts a variety of special events and exhibitions, as well as weddings, teas, and luncheons for individuals and organizations. Every autumn, it joins its neighbors in the annual Heritage Hill Tour of Homes, welcoming visitors who come from far and wide to marvel at the wonderful work accomplished by the preservationists and homeowners in the area.

Voigt House has been, as pointed out in the celebration of its Centennial Year in 1995-96, "Home for One Hundred Years," and as any owner of a vintage home will recognize, the need for maintenance and preservation work is

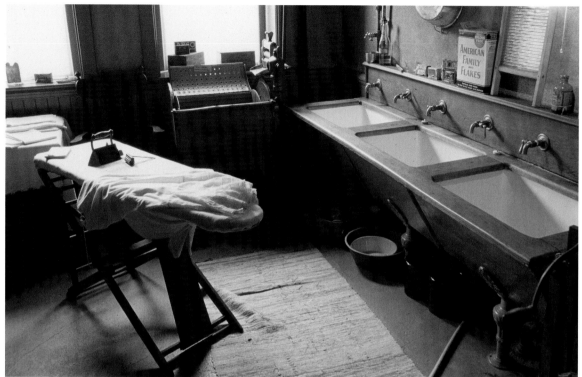

never-ending. Since assuming responsibility for Voigt House in 1989, the Public Museum of Grand Rapids has raised and invested more than $2.1 million to stabilize the home and preserve its unique historic contents.

In the Spotlight

As the decade of the 1970s began, the Public Museum was racing along, growing by leaps and bounds and attracting attention nationally as one of the country's urban museum success stories. In May 1970, the first Michigan Historic Preservation Conference was held in Grand Rapids, co-sponsored by the National Trust for Historic Preservation and 13 local and state organizations, including the Grand Rapids Public Museum. At the conference, it was announced that the Public Museum would be part of the first group of institutions to be evaluated by the American Association of Museums, a national organization founded in 1906, for a new program of accreditation that would signify that a museum had met national standards

established by the museum profession.

The accreditation program began with a study of American museums requested by President Lyndon B. Johnson in 1967. In a letter to the Chairman of the Federal Council on the Arts and Humanities, Johnson recognized America's 5,000 museums as precious cultural and educational resources, writing that their staffs and facilities contributed immeasurably to the nation's life and to educational advancement at all levels. He also acknowledged a dramatic increase in American museum attendance and the strain many budgets and facilities were showing, and requested a study to examine the situation.

America's Museums: The Belmont Report, named for the Smithsonian Conference Center in Maryland where the study group met, pointed out, among other needs, that museums must become more closely associated and coordinated in their efforts. The need for museum accreditation was especially pressing, and the American Association of Museums acted quickly to set up a small committee of museum professionals to consider the matter and arrive at a plan. The group, which included GRPM Director W.D. Frankforter, met from 1968-1970 in a variety of locations around the country. Toward the end of the committee's work, it

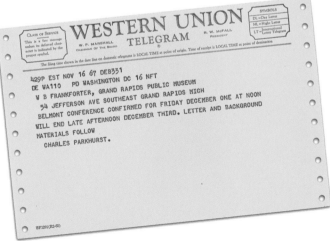

became apparent that what was needed was a test case. "Since the group had not met in Grand Rapids," wrote Frankforter in a 1971 article, "and because of the great diversity of subject matter covered by the Grand Rapids Public Museum, we were asked to be 'it'."

Accreditation was announced at AAM's annual conference in Denver during June 1971. Among the 16 institutions awarded accreditation with the Grand Rapids Public Museum were the Los Angeles County Museum of Natural History in California, the Henry Francis duPont Winterthur Museum in Delaware, the Andrew Dickson White Museum

of Art at Cornell University in New York, the Solomon R. Guggenheim Museum in New York City, the New York Botanical Garden in New York, and the Amon Carter Museum of Western Art in Texas. "Although no distinction was made regarding when they were accredited," wrote Frankforter, "we have the satisfaction of knowing that the Grand Rapids Public Museum was the first, and probably received as critical an inspection as any museum will ever have."

In 2004, approximately 750 of the nation's nearly 16,000 museums had achieved accreditation, according to the American Association of Museums.

ABOVE: **Second from right: W.D. Frankforter, Director of the Grand Rapids Public Museum, at a meeting in December, 1967 of a group appointed in response to a request by President Lyndon B. Johnson for a study on the condition and needs of American museums. The group met for two lengthy conferences at Belmont, a Maryland country estate, and their report became known as The Belmont Report.**

Pause for Reflection

Buoyed by the success of the Planetarium, Nature Center and Gaslight Village projects, as well as the national recognition of its peers, the Public Museum turned its attention to another challenge: the long-neglected Norton Indian Mounds, a group of extraordinary earthworks south of the city constructed by a civilization that flourished in the Grand River valley and across the Midwest 2,000 years ago.

Putting together funding from federal and state sources, the Museum developed a plan for a park and interpretive center at the Norton Mounds site, which had been named a National Historic Landmark in 1965. Through 1973 and 1974, the Museum continued with preliminary site development. Working with the Grand Rapid Inter-Tribal Council and other groups, the Museum sought a plan that the Native American and scientific communities could

agree upon. Dedication of the site was planned for October 1974, with dignitaries including Michigan Governor William Milliken invited.

As the date approached, work on the site was deemed inadequate, and the dedication was postponed. By the spring of 1975, it was clear that there were many other issues surrounding not only the Norton Mounds project, but the collection and exhibition policies of the Public Museum, reflecting concerns that were being raised by Native Americans nationwide. Vociferous debates in Board of Art & Museum Commissioners and City Commission meetings, and in the local media, centered on Native American culture, traditions and spiritual burial practices.

Although efforts were made to establish an advisory committee to address issues and resolve concerns, even that was not accomplished until 1976. Plans for the development of the Norton Mounds were put on hold, indefinitely. In the early years of the 21st century the Public Museum reopened the discussion by initiating the Norton Mounds National Historic Landmark Cultural Resources Project, continuing a longstanding interest in the original inhabitants of the Grand River valley, which is the subject of the next chapter of this book.

7. A Native American View of Time

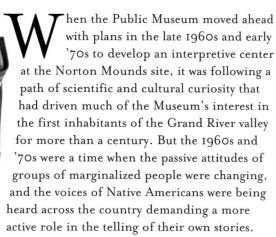

When the Public Museum moved ahead with plans in the late 1960s and early '70s to develop an interpretive center at the Norton Mounds site, it was following a path of scientific and cultural curiosity that had driven much of the Museum's interest in the first inhabitants of the Grand River valley for more than a century. But the 1960s and '70s were a time when the passive attitudes of groups of marginalized people were changing, and the voices of Native Americans were being heard across the country demanding a more active role in the telling of their own stories.

To the archaeologists and anthropologists examining what they called the Hopewell people, there was a distinct separation between the mound builders of 2000 years ago and the Anishinabek, descendants of the Native Americans living in the valley when the first European settlers arrived. But there are other ways of looking at time.

In his book, *A Forest of Time: American Indian Ways of History*, University of California professor Peter Nabokov explores motivations and practices through which American Indians have remembered their diverse past. In his introduction, he explains his title, "adapted from Chippewa historian David Beaulieu's issue with the European model of history, which he analogized as 'a (Euro-American) tree with many different branches, the idea of variations on a common theme,'" writes Nabokov. "In its place, Beaulieu proposed a more egalitarian alternative that he, in turn, attributed to Navajo historian Ruth Roessel, 'a forest of many different and varied trees,' with its stand of independent tribal approaches to recollecting and using the past."

Stephen E. Weil, former official of the Smithsonian Institution in Washington, D.C. and well-known writer about museums frequently quoted in this history, wrote in his 1995 book *A Cabinet of Curiosities*, "To understand the power of metaphor, not merely to express but to shape our thought, consider two very different ways in which we might think about time. In some cultures, time is understood through linear metaphors. It flows like a stream from here to there. Like a stream it must have a Beginning, a source, and, once it reaches its destination, an end as well ... there are other cultures that express themselves about time in metaphors that are cyclical instead of linear. Time, as thus envisioned, is a great circle ... other matters become important: the pattern of the seasons, the rhythm of repeated events, the

Many of the objects in the Public Museum's Native American collections came from early settlers interested in preserving the rare and beautiful works, and from local families. Public Museum Curator Christian Carron said in a 2003 interview that many of the best examples of early Anishinabek artifacts are in museums in Europe and the Vatican. "When those things were available, American institutions weren't developed yet," he explained. "Europeans were trading for or looting those things and taking them back. We have extraordinary things representing the Anishinabek, but given to us by Anishinabek families who wanted their stories to be told. It's a different way to collect, and a different way the community feels about us because of that."

OPPOSITE: One of the most extraordinary objects in the Public Museum's Native American collections is a rare trade-cloth and bead pouch. The shoulder bag, ca. 1897, is Potawatomi, made of wool and glass beads, and was the gift of Mrs. J. Langdon McKee. It is part of *Anishinabek: The People of This Place* permanent exhibition at Van Andel Museum Center. The Museum also is fortunate to possess photographs taken at a street fair in Grand Rapids in 1897, showing a young Indian woman wearing the bag, as well as one with the unidentified girl posing with a woman in Victorian mourning clothes, identified as Mrs. Thos. D. Gilbert (LEFT). The photographs are signed "compliments Mr. Heath, Artist."

RIGHT: **Dr. Ezra S. Holmes, an active member of the Kent Scientific Institute for more than 40 years in the latter part of the 19th century and early years of the 20th, is pictured at the Norton Mounds in an undated photograph. Dr. Holmes died in 1915.**

BELOW: **W.B. Coffinberry, a founding member of the Grand Rapids Lyceum of Natural History, was an avid amateur archaeologist. He led the KSI exploration of the Norton Mounds in 1874.** Photograph courtesy Grand Rapids History & Special Collections Center, Archives, Grand Rapids Public Library.

resonance between a time past and its reappearance in a time still to come."

The presence of the past. The consciousness of that is perhaps one of the most powerful attractions that Native American culture holds for those whose ideas about the past have been shaped in a more linear fashion, and, not surprisingly, has been a major interest of the Public Museum for 150 years.

Early Enthusiasm

When the first Europeans came to the Grand River valley, there were 30-40 earthen mounds on the west bank of the river, near the heart of what is now downtown Grand Rapids. Other mounds were scattered around the area, including a group noted with typically keen curiosity by John Ball, a founder in 1854 of the Grand Rapids Lyceum of Natural History, forerunner to the Public Museum. In his diaries for fall 1836, journaling his explorations seeking land for Eastern investors, he wrote, "In exploring the Ottawa land the last time, we were in the woods about a week, and coming out we stopped

at Ezra Chubb's, on his farm in a log cabin between Grandville and Grand Rapids, on whose place near the Grand River are some Indian mounds as well defined as I have ever seen."

Many of the downtown mounds were razed in the 1850s for the grading of streets. "It was a project of cutting down or filling up," wrote Charles E. Belknap, a Civil War hero, mayor of the city and representative to the U.S. Congress, in his 1922 book *The Yesterdays of Grand Rapids*. "And so the Indian mounds, with their historic contents, were carted away to fill the low places." But in 1874, wrote Belknap, a committee led by Wright L. Coffinberry, another of the Lyceum's founders, undertook an exploration of "many of the 47 mounds then remaining in and about the Rapids." Accompanying him was Superintendent of Schools E.A. Strong, who was instrumental in bringing together the Lyceum and the Grand Rapids Scientific Club to form the Kent Scientific Institute, and was Director of KSI's Museum.

Wright L. Coffinberry was a noted antiquarian, amateur archaeologist, and a civil engineer for the City of Grand Rapids. Charged by the KSI board with exploration of the Norton Mound Group, Coffinberry and his colleagues excavated seven of the 17 mounds in a group three miles south of Grand Rapids named for the property owner, Captain A.N. Norton. The results of their exploration were presented in a report to a meeting of the American Association for the Advancement of Science in Detroit in 1875. A number of the objects found in the project were loaned for a display on prehistoric materials from Michigan included as part of the state's exhibit at the 1876 Centennial Exposition in Philadelphia.

Documentation of the events that followed is sketchy. In the first Annual Report of the Art & Museum Commission, May, 1918, Professor Strong wrote what has become the accepted story of the original Museum mounds collection: "All who visited the exposition from the state were well satisfied with the way in which the collection was displayed, but at the close of the exposition, just before the material was to be packed and returned, the case was broken open in the night and every object removed. Not one was ever recovered. The collection was especially rich in copper objects ... hollow ware, and large sea shells suitable for holding water." In a report to the State Centennial Board of Managers, published in Detroit, 1876, the Kent Scientific Institute is credited with sending "One hundred and thirty specimens" to the Philadelphia Exposition.

In the archives of the Public Museum, however, is a handwritten, undated inventory submitted by E.A. Strong ("of Centennial Committee") titled "K.S.I. Centennial Exhibit. Articles broken, missing, &c." in which it seems that not all that was sent was unreturned. Of 60 arrowheads, 53 returned, of 12 copper articles sent, 9 returned. "Bone Articles. 8 Spears, lances, stilettos & handles sent, 7 returned. The

LEFT: Handwritten, undated inventory submitted by E.A. Strong, perhaps a clue to items missing from the 1876 Centennial Exposition in Philadelphia.

missing one was not important." What was lost, and where it ended up, remains a Museum mystery.

In 1915, KSI Director Herbert Sargent carried out another formal excavation of the Norton Mounds. Although in his report on the project, he wrote that "One of the prime reasons of mound investigation is to secure objects of interest," the KSI Museum had recently been the recipient of a number of artifacts assembled, according to Sargent, by Mr. Claude Hamilton and representing "distinctively Kent County Mound Builders." Hundreds of the artifacts, including flint spears and arrows, stone hammers, pipes, copper implements, and

RIGHT: Bible translated into the Potawatomi language, used at the Slater Mission established in 1827 by the American Baptist Missionary Union for the Ottawa Indians on the Grand River. It was one of the first European settlements in what is now Grand Rapids and for almost ten years was the only school. The Bible was printed by Packard & Van Benthuysen Printers of Albany, New York, 1833. It is shown as part of the exhibition *Anishinabek: The People of This Place* at Van Andel Museum Center, 2003.

BELOW: Quilled bark canoe, believed to have been made by the son of Chief Petoskey, after whom the city of Petoskey, Michigan is named. The presentation canoe was made as a gift for Daniel C. Lamberton, a Grand Rapids resident, in return for his help during a Petoskey family illness, ca. 1880.

beads were "at present on exhibition" at the KSI Museum that was opened in the Howlett House in 1904. More valuable to the Museum, wrote Sargent, "is the acquiring of information which will show the way in which mound building was performed, to give a fair conjecture as to the motives actuating the people in performing this work, and if possible to acquire information regarding the social customs of the people themselves."

Although Sargent's intentions were good, his scientific training was not in archaeology, and his records were not adequate to determine if he met any of his goals. It would be 50 years before the Museum would again pursue a scientific interest in the culture of the earliest Grand River valley inhabitants.

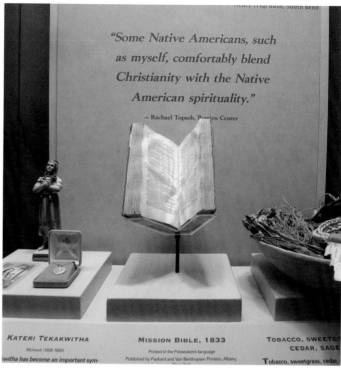

"*Some Native Americans, such as myself, comfortably blend Christianity with the Native American spirituality.*"
— Rachael Topash, Berrien Center

KATERI TEKAKWITHA
Mohawk (1656-1680)
...witha has become an important sym-

MISSION BIBLE, 1833
Printed in the Potawatomi language
Published by Packard and Van Benthuysen Printers, Albany,

TOBACCO, SWEETG...
CEDAR, SAGE
Tobacco, sweetgrass, cedar,

Objects of Interest

The Public Museum has become an important repository for objects that trace not only the history of Native American culture in the region, but also the interaction between successive settlers. From a Bible translated into the Potawatomi language used at the Slater Mission in the earliest days of the settlement of Grand Rapids, to a splint basket made by Ottawa Indians near Eastmanville and given to John Ball shortly after the founding of the Lyceum in 1854, to more than 300 American Indian baskets assembled by Robert Y. Spier during travels throughout the country and donated to the Museum by Mrs. Speir in 1948, the Museum's collection teems with rare and beautiful objects that speak to rich Native American cultures.

But it was not objects that drove the next wave of interest in the Norton Mounds site. Over the years it became the property of the City of Grand Rapids, and some attempts to develop

it into a public park were occasionally put forward, but the Mounds remained largely forgotten. Weldon D. Frankforter became Assistant Director of the Public Museum in 1962, when plans were in the works for a new freeway connecting Grand Rapids and Holland. Much to the dismay of the newly arrived paleontologist, the proposed route of I-196 ran straight through the Norton Mounds site, threatening once again to raze a sacred burial ground in the path of road building. In a 1974 *Grand Rapids Press* profile,

he recounted his first visit to the mounds three months after arriving in the city. "Would you believe there was a right-of-way stake for the highway," he asked incredulously, "... right in the middle of one of the mounds?" Frankforter contacted Fred See, Superintendent of Parks for the city, and the two convinced the "highway people" to move the route.

Working with the local Archaeological Society (named for Wright Coffinberry), Frankforter helped to launch a new scientific

ABOVE: **The Norton Indian Mounds, now a National Historic Landmark, are on the east bank of the Grand River, just south of Grand Rapids. In the undated aerial photo above, looking across the river from the west, they're in the wooded area at the center.**

investigation of the Norton Mounds. The committee raised funds for a two-year project by the University of Michigan Museum of Anthropology, under the direction of Dr. James Griffin, in 1963-64. The studies, along with the site's brush with near-destruction, revitalized interest in the Mounds as a public treasure. The Indian Mounds Park Development Committee, with W.D. Frankforter as Secretary, applied to the National Park Service Committee on Historic Sites and Buildings, and in October 1965 Senator Phil Hart announced in Washington, D.C. that the Norton Indian Mounds was named a National Historic Landmark, the highest status the U.S. can bestow on a historic site.

In May 1970 the Norton Mounds were transferred from the City of Grand Rapids Parks Department to the Public Museum and in 1971 a Historic Preservation grant from the National Park Service was awarded for restoration of the site. Plans were in the works for a visitor center, parking lot, exhibitions, pathways and more. An advocacy group with both Native and non-Native participants was formed to assist.

During the 1970s, however, the American Indian civil rights movement was having an effect on the local community. In a report assembled in 2003 by a team working on the Norton Mounds Cultural Resource Project, Debra Muller, the Project Manager, wrote that attitudes in the Native American community at the time were changing. "A cultural rebirth had begun that rekindled the self-identity and self-empowerment that had been latent in the recent past," she explained. "Apathetic attitudes were changing."

In addition to protests about development plans for the Norton Mounds site, local Native American groups were concerned that the Museum had on display human remains and artifacts from earlier excavations. Although some in the community had differing views, many united behind issues of repatriation and inclusion, and by 1975 petitions were being circulated by the Young Native Americans of the Grand Rapids Inter-Tribal Council, the Grand Valley American Indian Lodge and individual Native American community members and supporters demanding that remains and artifacts be removed from display and returned for reburial.

By this time the controversy was becoming public. Meetings of the Board of Art & Museum Commissioners and the City Commission were the scene of heated exchanges, and a group of young Native Americans met for a clean-up and barricaded the Mounds site. A resolution to remove all human remains from display was passed by the Board of Art & Museum Commissioners (predating federal legislation on the issue by some 15 years), and plans for further development of the Norton Mounds were put on hold. The Museum established a Native American Advisory Committee to consider the mounds site, as well as help in planning for a new permanent exhibition at the Museum, with the working title *Man in the Lower Grand River Valley*. Although the Norton Mounds would recede from the public spotlight for another 25 years, while remaining under the protection of the Public Museum, the new exhibition would include the story of the Hopewell people as part of a 10,000 year saga of human activity in the Grand River valley.

People of the Grand

When the Museum staff first began to plan a new exhibition tracing the development of human life along the Grand River, it was slated to be part of the celebration of the 1976 Bicentennial of the U.S. and Sesquicentennial of the city of Grand Rapids. The project, like many Museum endeavors, grew exponentially in scope and complication. Most of the work and research for the exhibition was done in-house, including activities such as growing special types of squash to cast for just the right exhibit props, and marshaling an army of volunteers to hand-fabricate every leaf for every tree in the dioramas. Some of the contacts made during the Norton Mounds excavation in the mid-1960s resulted in assistance from a variety of professional advisors including Dr. Richard Flanders, who had been the field supervisor for the University of Michigan project, and was now teaching at Grand Valley State College, with the ample resource of student researchers at his disposal.

A sneak preview of the exhibition was offered as part of the Museum's 125th anniversary open house in November 1979. "People are anxious," said Curator of Exhibits Carl Ulanowicz in a *Grand Rapids Press* article. "They're looking through the door." Ulanowicz joined the Public Museum staff in 1976 just as the project was getting off the ground, and supervised its fabrication and installation.

People of the Grand, tracing the history of human habitation in the area from the Ice Age to 1826, when the first Europeans settled, opened to the public in November 1980. "We rationalized that the actual American Revolu-

tion only started in 1776. It lasted to 1789," quipped staff artist Bob Bushewicz in a 2004 interview. "We finally finished the hall in 1980 and declared that it was done ahead of schedule!"

The project took a major portion of the Museum staff's time for more than five years, as well as assistance from a number of volunteers. But there were other activities during that period that related to the research and development work for the exhibition. In 1975 *Other Voices*, an exhibition of paintings of Sioux Indians by

local artist Paul Collins, was a fundraiser for a scholarship fund for Indian students, along with the sale of the catalog of the exhibit.

In 1976, Museum Assistant Director Gordon Olson led the Upper Great Lakes Indian Trade Bead Research Project, a joint effort with the Cranbrook Academy of Art/Museum in Bloomfield Hills, Michigan, to identify trade beads in collections in Michigan and establish a sequential typology. An exhibi-

ABOVE: *People of the Grand* **was originally planned to open with a large mural depicting two Paleo-Indians as a backdrop for the Museum's huge mastodon skeleton. The ambitious project immediately ran into problems. "First shot out of the box," wrote staff artist and chief preparator Robert Bushewicz in an informal history of his nearly 20-year career at the Public Museum, "Gary Fraser (who worked for the Museum from 1974-2004) started to dismantle our mastodon and it was found to have deteriorated more in the century in our urban atmosphere than it had in at least 10,000 years in the Moorland swamps. So back to the drawing board." They made a cast of a mastodon's skull and positioned it in a diorama as it might have been found, based on notes from the original excavation.**

LEFT: Opening ceremonies for the temporary exhibition *Archaeology Here and There* **on February 7, 1971, featured dancing by, from left, Renee Peters, Warren Bosin, Ronald Crow, Doug Bosin, and Ike Peters. The exhibition was co-sponsored by the Wright L. Coffinberry Chapter of the Michigan Archaeological Society and included 5000 years of Native American artifacts, featuring traditional clothing loaned by William Thatcher, president of the United Tribes of Michigan.**

ABOVE: **Native American activities were popular at the annual** *Pioneer Days* **at the Public Museum in the 1970s and 1980s.**

BELOW: **A major research project resulted in a publication and traveling exhibition.**

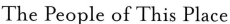

tion titled *Beads: Their Use by Upper Great Lakes Indians* was organized and toured eight Midwest museums. The catalog of the exhibition was published by the Museum Association and a Super-8 film showing beadmaking and beadworking techniques was produced. In 1979, Museum staff set up three exhibit cases showing Indian beadwork of the Upper Great Lakes at the first (and since annual) *Homecoming of the Three Fires Pow Wow* in the new city park named *Ah-Nab-Awen* (the resting place) on the west bank of the river in downtown Grand Rapids.

The People of This Place

When work began on exhibition planning for a new riverfront Public Museum in the 1980s, it was first envisioned that a permanent exhibition titled *The People of This Place* would be an in-depth study of change and continuity in human society over thousands of years. "Who were the ancient

people?," wrote consultant James E. Sims in an Exhibition Master Plan draft dated March 1989, "is a way of asking about all origins of time." The landscape, and its "succession of life forms and human settlements" would be "treated in chronological sequence."

But the team working on the planning also was exploring a new approach to community involvement that was gaining ground in museum circles. "Partnership between the museum and the community is what educators and museum professionals call 'audience advocacy,'" wrote Erik Alexander, a Curator at the Public Museum from 1989-2003, in an April 1993 article for the newsletter *Discoveries*. In meetings of the advisory committee formed to help develop the new project, wrote Alexander, Native Americans advised Museum curators that the exhibition should not be a description of "another" culture from the viewpoint of historians and anthropologists, and that the materials should not be presented in traditional 'time-line' or geographic arrangements common in exhibits about Native Americans. What the exhibition should, and does, contain are the stories of people, past and present, along with treasured objects from the Museum's collections.

The exhibition project team, with sound and video consultants led by producer Lorraine Schmidt, traveled throughout West Michigan in the summer of 1992, conducting nearly a hundred taped interviews. The result was "an opportunity for Michigan Indians to speak for themselves on topics ranging from experiences of growing up Indian to politics, spirituality, art, social issues, or just about any subject the individual cared to discuss," wrote Bryan Kwapil, the Museum's Curator of Collections from 1987-1996, in the March 1993 *Discoveries*. The result was "a remarkable portrait of a unique and rich West Michigan culture," wrote Kwapil, that permeates the Van Andel Museum Center exhibition which opened in June 1995.

Millennium Mounds

In September, 2002, Museum Director Timothy J. Chester announced the Norton Mounds Cultural Resource Research Project, a process beginning then to document the site and plan for its future management. "The Public Museum of Grand Rapids has quietly guarded and cherished this ancient and sacred burial ground for more than a century," he wrote in the newsletter *Discoveries*. "(It) is about to be studied and assessed with an eye to its long-term preservation."

The impetus for the project was a proposal to create a 1500-acre park straddling several city boundaries along the Grand River, and encompassing the Norton Mounds site. In 1998, a board was appointed by the City of Grand Rapids and Kent County to work with a national council supporting year 2000-2001 projects to celebrate the millennium. A park was unanimously approved in January 2000 as a project

that would have long-lasting impact on the community.

The project also would have an impact on the Public Museum. "At times, I've become disheartened about the lack of respect shown for this important sacred burial ground and the adjacent riverfront wetlands," wrote Chester, who became Director of the Museum in 1988. "But the Museum has always had faith that,

sooner or later, the time would come to tell the story of the Hopewell Indians, and reconsider the Norton Mounds' visibility. Now, with the advent of the adjacent Millennium Park, increased public access is inevitable and it's time to decide how best to preserve the site while managing that access."

Funded by a federal historic preservation grant through the Michigan Department of Transportation, and supplemented with funds provided by the Public Museum's governing board, the Norton Mounds Cultural Resource Research Project was launched, and Project Manager Debra Muller brought on staff. A citizen of the Nottawaseppi Huron Band of Potawatomi, with a background in business, public service and administration, Muller brought a refreshing perspective to the process. After meeting with representatives from tribal and Native American groups around the state, as well as the National Park Service, Smithsonian Institution, Kent County Parks, archaeology experts, and others who have a stake in the ways the site will be preserved and made accessible, she led a series of *Community Conversations* in the fall of 2003 and winter of 2004. "The Museum has looked to the community for answers first," she explained in a

September 2003 newsletter article. "That's how Native Americans are comfortable, working in circles, that's the true democracy. All voices, all opinions are heard."

The Museum also commissioned the Commonwealth Cultural Resources Group of Jackson, Michigan to prepare a description and history of the landmark. Their report detailed the physical and cultural background of the site; cultural resources nearby; the history, archaeology and collections related to the mounds; the context and significance of the mound group; and contained a section on Anishinabek perspectives, a summary, and recommendations.

A community advisory council of interested citizens and representatives of government, academic, and stakeholder organizations was formed for the project, and will decide on a recommended course of action based on the research and community input. "The Park is happening, period," said Muller in the newsletter article. "Preservation by not being accessible is no longer an option."

Christian G. Carron, Curator of the Public Museum, was also quoted in the same article. "The Museum doesn't have any agenda other than to preserve, protect, and educate," he explained. "But few people realize what we have here, how important it is that these structures exist. Think about how far people travel to see Stonehenge, the Mayan temples, the pyramids. These have international significance."

RIGHT: Artifacts recovered from University of Michigan excavations in 1963-64, including pottery shards preserved in the Museum's collections, have played a central role in understanding the early people of western Michigan. In a 2003 report by the Commonwealth Cultural Resources Group, Inc. for the Norton Mounds National Historic Landmark Cultural Resource Research Project, an analyst wrote, "Simply put, because of those excavations it is difficult to make any statements about Middle Woodland peoples in the region without some reference to the Norton Mounds data."

8. A Cabinet of Wonder on the River: 1977-1994

When John Ball and his friends first came together in the middle of the 19th century to form what would become the Public Museum of Grand Rapids, much of their interest was in sharing the private collections they had amassed in their travels and wide-ranging scholarly pursuits. These collections of artifacts, oddities, and specimens of natural history, known as *Wunderkammer* or Cabinets of Wonder or Curiosity, had become the rage in Europe in the centuries following the discovery of the New World. Learned gentlemen of the 17th and 18th centuries, much more ecumenical in their interests than the specialists of today, often acquired and maintained large and diverse private repositories of fossils, rocks and minerals, preserved specimens of flora and fauna, relics of ancient cultures, oddities of nature, and anything that struck their fancy as worth further investigation.

Inevitably, the collections began to outgrow the homes of their owners, who also had a natural desire to compare and discuss their treasures with others, and eventually make the collections available for public display.

More than a hundred years after Ball and the others founded the Lyceum of Natural History, the Grand Rapids Public Museum was

outgrowing its capacity to maintain and display the enormous collections that had blossomed from those original Cabinets of Wonder. In 1976, the Museum purchased its first building solely dedicated to collections storage, a building on State Street just southeast of the main Museum that came to be known as the 'Attic'. Ironically, it was the same building that Frank DuMond had leased some 40 years earlier to house the Museum more economically for three years during the Depression. The former Nash garage and showroom was the Museum Director's inspiration for the 'Grand Rapids

No one was more instrumental in making the Van Andel Museum Center (OPPO-SITE) possible than Steele Taylor (LEFT), who led the campaign for the building and served as president of the Board of Art & Museum Commissioners from 1984-2002. The Public Museum not only benefited from his business experience and volunteer dedication, but also from his personal interest in history and collecting. Exhibitions such as *I is for Ivory*, and *P is for Pewter* include examples of his acumen as a collector and generosity as a donor. Even as a boy, his eye for history must have been sharp. Photographs he took at age 11 on a trip to Berlin with his father, along with pages from his diary, lent a local aspect to *The Nazi Olympics: Berlin 1936*, a traveling exhibition that was the first circulated by the U.S. Holocaust Memorial Museum, and premiered at the Public Museum in 1998. In 2004, Steele Taylor was serving as Vice President of the Board of Art & Museum Commissioners, and a member of the Board of Directors of the Public Museum of Grand Rapids Friends Foundation, which he founded.

plan' Museum building that opened at 54 Jefferson in 1940.

But that facility, and the East Building addition acquired in 1958, were both bursting at the seams with 120 years of collecting. The new storehouse would address some problems temporarily, but it was clear that a long-term solution for better access and display was needed. The Museum once again launched into the process of planning and constructing a new museum building.

Planning for Another New Museum

In 1977, a Museum Planning Committee was organized with representatives from the city's Board of Art & Museum Commissioners and the Museum Association, staff from the Museum, and a liaison from the City Manager's office. A previous plan had been developed in the late 1960s for a joint project with the Grand Rapids Art Museum to create a Museum Block on the Jefferson/Fulton site, but years of work came to nought when attention and funding turned to urban renewal in the center city. The inclination of most was that the best spot for a successful new Museum would be a move closer to the heart of the city.

One of the committee members was a newly appointed member of the Board of Art & Museum Commissioners, Steele A. Taylor. A native of New Jersey, Taylor had come to Grand Rapids in 1948, and had become a respected businessman and active community volunteer. "I loved museums and as soon as I came to town I had gone to ours," he remembered in a 2004 interview. "That old building had become a clunker. Some of the exhibits were really well done, but you couldn't do anything with it." He joined the Board of Art & Museum Commissioners in 1976. "When I was appointed I said what are you doing about the future of this place?" he recalled ruefully. "They put me in charge of planning."

By 1979 it became clear that staffing would be

needed for the project, and the committee applied to the Grand Rapids Foundation for funding to open an office and hire a coordinator.

Mary Esther Lee had been a docent at the Public Museum since 1972, and was part of the Docentry League's leadership. She was president of the Museum Association and had been a

member of the original long-range planning committee, which was largely volunteer driven. In 1979, the committee appointed her as Planning Coordinator. "We had an office in the Early People Hall," Lee remembered in a 2004 interview. "There was a thin wall between the mummy and other ancient stuff and our office. There was me and a volunteer secretary, and we had a huge graphic on the wall outlining 17 subcommittees and a timeline."

It was not the best of times to be launching a major building campaign. In 1980, General Motors had its worst year in history, and the U.S. government saved Chrysler Corporation from bankruptcy with a $1.5 billion bailout. The state budget director of Michigan called the economic outlook "bleak." By September 1982, the U.S. jobless rate was 10.1%, the highest in 42 years.

But the Museum Planning Committee forged ahead. Following a series of community forums, surveys and consultation, a search was conducted for a planning team. In 1980, E.

Verner Johnson & Associates of Boston was selected to develop a master plan. The firm had recently completed projects for the South Carolina State Museum, the Heard Museum in Phoenix, and the South Quadrangle of the Smithsonian Institution in Washington, D.C.

As the planning process advanced, the economic climate was taking its toll on the city's budget. Close on the heels of a gala celebration of the Museum's 125th anniversary in November 1979, severe restrictions in Museum funding had led to the loss of staff, including the elimination of the Visual Education Division. In February 1981, for the first time in its history, an admission fee was initiated. By the end of fiscal year 1982, nearly half the staff had been laid off, including all part-time employees, and the Museum closed on Saturdays.

But, as always, the remaining staff, and hundreds of volunteers, soldiered on. The long-awaited exhibition *People of the Grand* opened, and Museum Director W.D. Frankforter organized a group of enthusiasts to begin a fundraising campaign to purchase a working carousel.

Inspired by a popular antique merry-go-round in the Children's Museum of Indianapolis, and community memories of a carousel at the old Ramona Park at Reeds Lake east of Grand Rapids, Frankforter was determined that the Public Museum would have one as the centerpiece of its new facility, wherever that might be. The first fundraiser, the *Carousel Waltz* in November 1981, featured the Lawrence Welk Orchestra and raised enough for a down payment on the purchase of a 1928 carousel from an amusement park in Barnesville, Pennsylvania. It was the beginning of a decade-plus process that would result in the magnificently restored, working carousel that now flies over the Grand River at Van Andel Museum Center (more about the carousel can be found later in this chapter).

It was a frustrating time for the Museum Planning Committee, however. After the presentation and approval of a comprehensive Master Plan in April 1982, the City Commission voted to make the Public Museum part of the West Bank Action Plan for development on the Grand River downtown. Jay Van Andel, co-founder and Chairman of the Board of Amway Corporation, had agreed to chair the capital campaign to raise the funds necessary to build the ambitious project. In June, supporters broke out the champagne for the hundreds of people who had participated in the planning process up to that point. It was a bit premature.

For the next five years, the Museum worked with the City of Grand Rapids as they attempted to develop the new building as part of a series of cooperative projects: as part of a downtown campus for Grand Valley State College along with a hotel, then as part of a massive Cultural Services Consolidation millage project including the Zoo and area libraries, turned down by Kent County voters in 1986. Finally, in 1987, an unpopular proposal put the Museum on Monroe Mall as part of a shopping/office complex.

"So much drama, exhilaration and heartbreak condensed into such a dry paragraph,"

OPPOSITE: **Mary Esther Lee came to West Michigan in 1971 with her husband, Noble Lee. Both became active with the Museum Association, and Mary Esther also served as a docent for eight years. Trained as a teacher, she was a part-time faculty member at Grand Rapids Junior College in 1979 when the Museum Planning Committee hired her to coordinate the planning project. She shepherded the fundraising campaign, and was project coordinator for design and construction for Van Andel Museum Center and its exhibitions and programming. "It was exciting," she exclaimed in a 2004 interview. "I was there when the whale was being reinstalled, and later at 2:00 a.m. when they hung the Driggs Skylark biplane. That's the payoff," she continued. "The joy of being in this job is working with creative people, part of a tag-team of people with expertise and excitement for what they do."**

"We would not have this Museum (VAMC) if it weren't for Mary Esther Lee," declared Nancy Douglas in a 2004 interview. "She kept it all on track and focused." Public Relations Director of the Museum from 1979-1984, Douglas also served on the Museum Friends Board, including a term as president, until 1999.

Lee became Development Officer for the Public Museum in 1992, and in 2004 was enthusiastically working with a group of volunteers on a campaign titled *150 years young* to raise $5.3 million for events, temporary and permanent exhibitions, and programs to celebrate the 150th anniversary of the Public Museum of Grand Rapids.

LEFT:: **Many of the new Museum building's 'icon objects' were funded through separate campaigns, including the 1928 Spillman Engineering Carousel.**

LEFT: When Timothy J. Chester arrived in 1986 to become the Assistant Director of the Public Museum, the situation was, as he described it in a 2004 interview, "challenging." After he was named Director of the Museum in 1988, he set out to change "a culture that was the result of years of 'we're moving, we're not moving,' over and over. Departments existed out of communication with each other," he explained. "We needed to learn how to pull together as a team. We used everything to learn new competencies—a new Museum shop, a new development office—as a dry run for the new Museum. We got training on working together in groups, on how to interact."

Chester is a native of Michigan, raised in St. Clair Shores before earning B.A. and M.A. degrees at the University of Michigan. A job at Greenfield Village & Henry Ford Museum during his first year of college led to his participation in a graduate program in museum studies at the University. "A group of the college-age guides at Greenfield Village were freshmen but we all decided this is what we wanted," he remembered in 2004. "Many of us still work in museums." Before a six-year stint at the Louisiana State Museum, he gained experience at the University's Museum of Art, the Corcoran Gallery of Art in Washington, D.C. and with the National Trust for Historic Preservation.

Chester became an active member of the community when he came to Grand Rapids, following in the footsteps of the civic-minded directors who preceded him. He serves on a number of local, state, and national boards and committees, including the Grand Rapids/Kent County Convention & Visitors Bureau, the Governor's Advisory Committee for the Michigan Department of History, Art & Libraries, and the Michigan Museums Association, the Association of Midwest Museums, and the American Association of Museums. He has been a consultant and grant reviewer for the National Endowment for the Humanities and the Institute of Museum & Library Services for many years.

BELOW: Jay Van Andel, center, and his daughter-in-law Carol Van Andel celebrate with Timothy Chester.

mused Mary Esther Lee in a 2004 interview after reading the summary of those years. "We'd hit this wall, we'd go back and re-do the plan. This didn't work, let's go around the block and take a different way. By the time we were done there were 150 volunteers—heads of large corporations working with stay-at-home moms—they believed in it and were dedicated for years and years. When we were down about some setback, I always said the same thing: No one will ever care about this as much as you do—if you give up, people will think that it isn't important and this will never happen."

But they did care, and they did do it, although it took another decade and more planning and fundraising than any other project in the city had ever mustered.

New Energy for a Renewed Effort

In January 1985, the Museum's Assistant Director, Richard Stryker, left to take a post in Texas, but not before making pointed comments to the local newspaper. He cited lack of city support for Museum activities, and declared that "For a museum this size, it's one of the worst facilities I've seen as far as preservation of objects is concerned."

A month before, in an article marking his 20th anniversary as Director, W.D. Frankforter also described a sad state of affairs. The Public Museum, which had led the country as the first accredited by the American Association of Museums in 1971, had been reaccredited in 1977. "I don't think we could get reaccredited today because of the condition of the museum," Frankforter lamented.

The Public Museum and the City of Grand Rapids were criticized for their handling of the search for a new Assistant Director, but, after a series of problems, Timothy J. Chester, Associate Director for Collections at the Louisiana State Museum in New Orleans, was hired in the summer of 1986.

In April 1988 W.D. Frankforter retired and

Chester was appointed acting director. After a national search, he was unanimously selected by the Board of Art & Museum Commissioners as Director of the Public Museum in September 1988. Board President Steele Taylor noted in *The Grand Rapids Press* that he had been especially impressed with Chester's skills in fund-raising and communication. "He's handled himself extremely well in this area of putting the new museum forward."

Taylor and the persistent members of the committee working on the plan for a new museum building had not been neglecting their own efforts toward that end. In 1986 a group met with Governor James Blanchard. "We put together a huge chart showing all the state arts funding," explained Taylor in a 2004 interview, "and over in the corner was a tiny little sliver, and that was what was going to West Michigan. The Governor said 'Don't show that chart again and we'll get you the $10 million.'"

It was the impetus needed for a flurry of fund-raising, a "huge period of time," according to Chester, "from 1989-1994 when that was all we did: planning and raising money." (Somewhere in there, however, time was found to change the name of the institution to the Public Museum of Grand Rapids, helping to define its identity, and for Deidra Edmond Mayweather, the Museum's Publications & Visitor Services Coordinator from 1985-2003, to launch *Museum* magazine.)

The Museum kicked off its capital campaign to raise $10 million in private funding in October 1989 (the goal was later raised to $12 million). *It's About Time*, seeking a third of the $30 million estimated cost of the project, was the largest single fundraising effort ever undertaken in West Michigan. "After years of effort, plans are about to become reality," wrote Jay Van Andel, chair of the campaign, in a letter to supporters. "The museum stands as a testament to ambitious plans and efforts by people of vision. Those of us who build this extraordinary and exciting museum will be remembered by the museum visitors of

the future. They'll know that we fulfilled our obligations to ensure that this institution will remain a collective and cultural memory that will never fade."

The obligation was fulfilled by community donors large and small: From people who paid $5 to sponsor a 5" blue rubber whale in races on the Grand River downtown, to school children collecting pennies, to the more than 19,000 people who donated at least $10 to "Write Your Name Into History" on commemo-

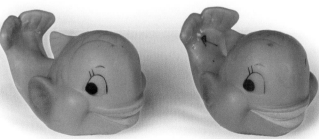

The races grossed approximately $50,000 each. But the second event also attracted unexpected attention to the city from a nationally syndicated columnist who happened to be lunching at the Amway Grand Plaza Hotel on September 21, 1991. Jeffrey Hart, a senior editor for the magazine *National Review* and former speechwriter for Ronald Reagan and Richard Nixon, wrote a column for King Features syndicated in nearly a hundred newspapers nationwide. He had seen from a window the capture of the tiny blue creatures in the river, and mistakenly thought it was a massive fish kill (a casual question to any of the participants might have set him straight). His column waxed eloquent about the "newly born fish, the sun glinting on their blue backs as they leaped and swam ... a joyful spectacle." He decried "the fish dumped like garbage on the banks of the river" and asked, "Do we really wish to be the sort of people who could perpetrate what I witnessed in Grand Rapids?"

Though Hart published a 'clarification' in which he bizarrely tried to justify his criticism, the story of his hilarious mistake was picked up across the country, including a story in the February 1992 issue of *Harper's* magazine titled "Hook, Line and Sinker."

ABOVE: "The ceremonial turning of dirt to signify the beginning of construction was experienced by thousands of onlookers with lumpy throats and wet eyes," wrote Museum Director Timothy Chester in the Fall 1991 issue of *Museum* magazine, describing groundbreaking for the new Museum Center on September 7, 1991.

Steele Taylor, pictured third from right, said in a 2004 interview that, without a doubt, it was his favorite moment in his decades as President of the Board of Art & Museum Commissioners and active Museum volunteer: "There was Gerry Ford, (former U.S. President, above fourth from left), the Governor (John Engler, above fourth from right), and me with my little spade and my speech. Putting that shovel into the ground—after all the work, the years and years—that was really it for me."

Pictured at the ceremony are, from left, Kenneth Kuipers, Chair of the Kent County Board of Commissioners; Gerald Helmholdt, Mayor of the City of Grand Rapids; Jay Van Andel, Chair of the Capital Campaign; President Ford, Governor Engler, Steele Taylor; U.S. Fifth District Congressman Paul Henry, and David Thompson, President of the Friends of the Public Museum.

RIGHT: Jay and Betty Van Andel present a $3 million check to the campaign, accepted on behalf of the Museum by Steele Taylor, President of the Board of Art & Museum Commissioners. The gift was the largest single donation made to a cultural organization in West Michigan at the time.

rative plaques at the new facility. The Steelcase Foundation made a $1 million grant in 1988, Grand Rapids Foundation followed in 1989 with $1 million. Peter & Pat Cook gave a $1 million grant that eventually funded the Cook Carousel Pavilion, and Meijer Theater honors a $500,000 gift from Fred & Lena Meijer (who also had helped to fund the restoration and re-installation of the whale). But it was the $3 million gift by Jay and Betty Van Andel in the spring of 1991, the largest donation in the Museum's history, that set the stage for a gala groundbreaking ceremony on September 7.

150 Years of Community Support

When Van Andel Museum Center opened on the Grand River downtown, it was not only a reflection of hard work by hundreds of volunteers, it was a testament to the thriving community West Michigan had become. The final total expenditure for the construction of the Museum Center, its exhibitions, furnishings, equipment, and parking ramp, was nearly $40 million. Ten million came from the State of Michigan, $7.4 million from Kent County's Hotel-Motel Tax Fund, $3.4 million from the Downtown Development Authority, and another $6 million plus from city, federal, and other sources and interest.

But by far the largest segment of the support for the massive project, the most ambitious ever undertaken in the area, came from private contributions, both financial and labor-intensive. As it has for 150 years, the Public Museum inspired the community to dig deep and work hard. Hundreds of volunteers worked to raise more than $12 million, and on teams restoring the spectacular major attraction artifacts that would be showcased in the new building, including a spectacular Theater Organ, a working steam engine, and the Carousel.

The Museum's building at 54 Jefferson had cost $208,901 in 1940 (approximately

$2.2 million in 1994 dollars, using Consumer Price Index comparisons). Its construction was financed by city and federal funds, but accomplished also with tremendous hands-on volunteer efforts by Museum supporters. The Museum's 150-year history is a steady progression of donor and volunteer involvement, beginning with the men whose collections, financial support, and curatorial services set the stage for an institution still primarily supported by its community.

In 1859, the Grand Rapids Lyceum of Natural History was meeting downtown in rooms rented on the fourth floor of the Luce Block, a large building on the corner of Monroe and Justice (now Ottawa), on the site where, in 2004, a new Grand Rapids Art Museum was under construction. The Lyceum also installed their library and collections there, but by the end of the year, membership dues were insufficient to pay the rent. At the Lyceum's annual meeting, John Ball donated a

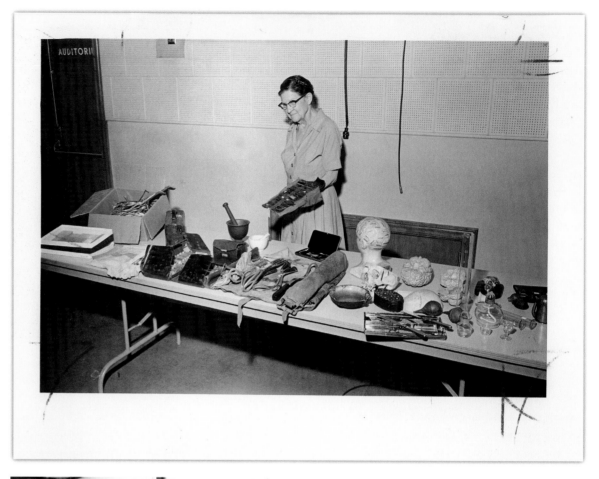

TOP RIGHT: Ruth Herrick was one of the first women to practice medicine in Kent County, an avid scholar, collector, and vice president of the Wright L. Coffinberry Chapter of the Michigan Archaeological Society. Her many interests included American primitives, Oriental and Dutch antiques, glassware, and Native American artifacts.

In 1951, while digging in the rubble of the Indiana Goblet & Tumbler Factory, which had burned in 1903, Dr. Herrick recovered a mass of glass shards that allowed her to identify and authenticate what became known as Greentown Glass. She published a book about it in 1959, and the collection was part of a private museum she maintained at her home in Lowell.

Dr. Herrick also worked with the Kent County Medical Society to establish a medical collection and exhibitions at the Public Museum in 1961. She is pictured here with some of the historic collection she donated as part of that project. In June 1974, Dr. Herrick was on her way home from a celebration of Greentown Glass in Indiana when she was killed in a car accident. She bequeathed her home, assets, and many of her massive collections to the Public Museum, a donation totaling approximately $70,000, the largest in the Museum's history to that date.

BOTTOM RIGHT: Many objects in the *G is for Glass* exhibition at Van Andel Museum Center carry the name of Dr. Ruth Herrick as donor, but more poignant are the 40 boxes of Greentown Glass shards (INSET) lovingly gathered by  Dr. Herrick, now carefully preserved on the shelves of the Community Archives & Research Center.

Greentown Glass

$50 gold watch to "replenish the treasury," which R.C. Luce accepted as payment.

Ball's donation, approximately $1070 in 21st century dollars, would today make him a member of the Public Museum's prestigious Carousel Society, which, in the spring of 2004, numbered nearly 200 significant donors. It's the Endowment arm of a membership list that had grown to more than 4,000 supporters in 2004.

A Museum Development Association was established in 1916 to encourage private support, and the Museum building at 54 Jefferson was made possible in the 1930s by funds donated from the estate of Estelle Provin, although not directly (covered in Chapter Four of this book). The Museum Association, organized in 1952, laid the groundwork for the membership organization that still supports the Museum today. Private funding was important both for the establishment of the Planetarium and the construction of Gaslight Village in the 1960s, but it was a bequest from Dr. Ruth Herrick in 1976 that demonstrated the difference a truly dedicated individual donor could make.

The economic history of the Public Museum over 150 years is a roller coaster of lean years of budget cuts and staff sacrifices, balanced by incredible spurts of growth and development. One factor that remains constant is the recognition by leaders in the community that the Museum is a critical piece of the total picture that makes Grand Rapids a great city in which to live. In 1988, the Public Museum Foundation of Grand Rapids was established with a gift from Steele Taylor, President of the Board of Art & Museum Commissioners, as a fiduciary agency for the building project, but also to address the long-term needs of the city's Museum.

At the ceremony in May 1993 marking the laying of the cornerstone for the new Museum, Taylor announced that the Jay and Betty Van Andel Foundation was making an additional $3 million gift to the Museum Foundation to support a new endowment fund. "I'm proud of the generosity and community spirit I've seen during this public fund-raising campaign and proud to be a part of the effort," wrote Jay Van Andel in a statement for the ceremony. In a letter placed in the cornerstone, he said that the endowment gift was made "in the spirit of enhancing the museum's power to bring history to life and enrich the lives of future generations."

The gift also was a challenge to create a substantial endowment fund for the Public Museum. The Carousel Society was formed in 1995, and many donors rose to meet the goal. After Van Andel Museum Center opened downtown, a great surge in support brought more than 2,000 new donors to the Museum's membership roster, and private funds have continued to help the Public Museum meet the challenges of unpredictable economic fluctuations.

The Museum's endowment fund has grown

with the help of many generous and thoughtful supporters, but some touch the heart just a little bit more. In 2003, Ardath Allen, a staff member at the Public Museum for nearly 30 years in the 1950s through the '70s, died and left all of her assets to the Public Museum of Grand Rapids Friends Foundation (as it became in 2003). She had previously made what Museum Director Timothy Chester called, in a February 2004 newsletter article, "an astounding, unexpected (and at the time, anonymous) six-figure gift in support of the construction of Van Andel Museum Center." Her dedication to the

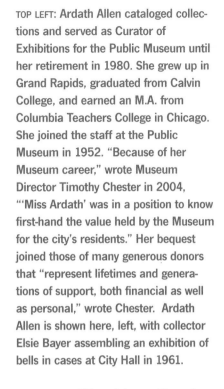

TOP LEFT: Ardath Allen cataloged collections and served as Curator of Exhibitions for the Public Museum until her retirement in 1980. She grew up in Grand Rapids, graduated from Calvin College, and earned an M.A. from Columbia Teachers College in Chicago. She joined the staff at the Public Museum in 1952. "Because of her Museum career," wrote Museum Director Timothy Chester in 2004, "'Miss Ardath' was in a position to know first-hand the value held by the Museum for the city's residents." Her bequest joined those of many generous donors that "represent lifetimes and generations of support, both financial as well as personal," wrote Chester. Ardath Allen is shown here, left, with collector Elsie Bayer assembling an exhibition of bells in cases at City Hall in 1961.

BOTTOM LEFT: Although large gifts and bequests are crucial to the long-term health of the Museum, the thousands of members and smaller donors who support the institution year after year are the foundation of its well-being. Pillars at the rotunda entrance to Van Andel Museum Center celebrate the more than 22,000 donors who made the building possible, including more than 19,000 who participated in the "Write Your Name Into History" project seeking donations of $10 or more. The list of names ranges across the demographic diversity of West Michigan, such as elementary school children who collected pennies in classrooms, and over 2,000 area educators who participated in a payroll deduction fund drive.

Museum, and frugal ways, resulted in a gift to the endowment of more than $1.3 million.

The New Museum

On November 19, 1994 Van Andel Museum Center opened to the public following the annual Santa Claus Parade that has heralded the beginning of the downtown holiday season for decades. More than 4,000 visitors flocked to the new Museum on its first day, twice the number that had been estimated. At a gala pre-

view the evening before, nearly 400 of the top donors to the campaign were feted in a black-tie event. Former U.S. President Gerald R. Ford reminisced about his fourth-grade trips to the city's old Public Museum building, his unsuccessful 1947 campaign to gain voter approval for a new museum, and his carefree carousel rides in Ramona Park. "Betty and I had a wonderful time," he told a *Grand Rapids Press* reporter. "It brought back a lot of memories for us ... this is a gem, a treasure, a magnificent facility."

The new Museum Center was designed to reflect the architectural heritage of West Michigan, incorporating

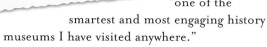

historically appropriate materials and details. Exterior bands of burnt orange and red brick set against cream was a common motif in 19th-century Grand Rapids, and also references the building traditions of Dutch immigrants. Situated directly on the river at the site of the old Voigt Crescent Flour Mill, the structure's mass celebrates its predecessor as well as the factories and mills that once lined both banks of the Grand River to harness its water power.

The Design Architect for the project was E. Verner Johnson & Associates, with Lawrence Man as Consulting Architect and Building Graphics Designer, and The WBDC Group/Beta Design Group, Grand Rapids architects. Exhibitions were designed by the PRD Group, Ltd. and their construction managed by Lee Perry.

A decade after its opening, Van Andel Museum Center continues to draw raves. In a 2003 *Grand Rapids Magazine* article about progressive new buildings in the city, one representative of the local chapter of the American Institute of Architects wrote that the personality of the city's newest buildings could be traced to the "daring —some would say outrageous—design" of Van Andel Museum Center, constructed a decade earlier. Readers of *On-The-Town*, West Michigan's arts and entertainment magazine, attested to the building's enduring popular appeal by voting it the area's Most Beautiful Building in the April 2003 'Townie' Awards poll. In the June/July 2004 issue of the magazine *American Heritage*, the author of a story about Grand Rapids described the Public Museum of Grand Rapids as "one of the smartest and most engaging history museums I have visited anywhere."

The new building was planned as an attractive facility for community use, and has served delightfully in that capacity during its first decade. The spacious riverside Galleria, along with the Cook Carousel Pavilion, the exhibition *Streets of Old Grand Rapids,* Meijer Theater, Chaffee Planetarium, and other Museum facilities, are popular sites for weddings, banquets, high school proms, corporate meetings and many other events. The Museum's Facility Use Department was established in 1994 by Felicia Betts. "Felicia worked very hard to create that department from scratch," remembered Museum Director Timothy Chester in a 2004 conversation. "Now it's a wonderful source of support and community involvement for the Museum." Felicia retired from the Museum in 2001, and her successor, Robert Vandermeer, has continued to build the department, earning the highest regard for catering services, both for special occasions and in The Museum Cafe, where food has become an important tool for the Museum's multi-

faceted approach to education. In 2004, the exhibition *Gratia Dei: A Journey Through the Middle Ages* prompted a carefully researched exploration of typical cuisine of the 14th and 15th centuries, offered in an authentic setting in The Olde World Cafe.

The Museum Center also was designed to take advantage of its riverfront location, the changing light reflected from the water and the view to and from the heart of the city across the open expanse. During the day huge windows frame spectacular views, and at night the Museum's key treasures are illuminated from within.

Clearly visible from outside the building are many of what the community has come to recognize as the Museum's 'icon objects:' the fin-back whale skeleton, undulating above the main gallery, as if somehow making its way up the river; the 1928 Spillman Carousel, suspended over the river in its own pavilion, a marvelous feat of engineering and sensitive design; the E. Howard tower clock from the 19th-century City Hall, torn down during the urban renewal fervor of the 1960s. Some objects acquired specifically for the new building have quickly assumed iconic status, including a giant Corliss-type steam engine built in 1905 that dramatically illustrates how early furniture factories were

LEFT: The first object installed in Van Andel Museum Center was a 30-foot long, Corliss-type steam engine weighing more than 70,000 pounds. In March 1993, it was lowered into the building to become part of the permanent exhibition *The Furniture City,* illustrating the steam engine as the source of power for the system of lineshafts, pulleys and belts that ran the furniture-making machines of the early 20th century.

The engine came from St. John's Table Company in Cadillac, located for the Public Museum by local furniture maker Carl Forslund, Jr. Made by Lane & Bodley of Cincinnati, it was installed there in 1905 when the factory was constructed. The Museum removed it in February 1991, with the help of West Shore Services of Allendale, and it was restored to operating condition by exhibit staff member Gary Fraser and a largely volunteer team coordinated by Larry Kelly, a Wyoming businessman and trustee of the Friends of the Public Museum.

INSET LEFT: Felicia Betts

OPPOSITE TOP: Celebrating at the preview gala that preceded the public opening of Van Andel Museum Center, (from left), former President Gerald R. Ford; Jay Van Andel, chair of the capital campaign for the new building, and (standing) Fred Meijer, a major donor to the project.

OPPOSITE BOTTOM: A 1955 photograph of Voigt Crescent Flour Mills, built on the west bank of the Grand River in the 19th century on the site where Van Andel Museum Center opened in 1994. It was owned by Carl G.A. Voigt, whose 19th-century home on College Avenue SE is now part of the Public Museum of Grand Rapids.

Many of the new Museum Center's "icon" objects were funded by separate campaigns led by tireless groups of enthusiasts. Peter Cook (LEFT), and Dave Mehney co-chaired the effort to raise funds to make a working antique carousel part of the Museum's new home. The idea was hatched in the late 1970s, when Museum Director W.D. Frankforter and Curator of Exhibits Carl Ulanowicz spent a glorious evening riding a carousel at the Children's Museum in Indianapolis. There also was considerable enthusiasm locally among people who remembered the old carousel at Ramona Park in East Grand Rapids. A dedicated group embarked on what would become a 12-year process, finally locating and purchasing a complete but dilapidated hand-carved wooden carousel in Barnesville, Pennsylvania, manufactured in 1928 by the Spillman Engineering Company.

John and Linda Layton of New Castle, Pennsylvania painstakingly repaired and restored the animals, chariots, and decorative panels of the carousel, working with Ulanowicz, who retired in 1998 after coordinating the project. The Wurlitzer band organ was restored by John Perschbacher, who had earlier restored the Museum's calliope.

Now acknowledged as one of the best restored carousels in the country, the Spillman flies above the Grand River, housed in the Cook Carousel Pavilion.

The Museum's Mighty Wurlitzer Theater Pipe Organ is an other example of the determination of a group of volunteers who responded to the call to secure a community treasure for the new Museum.

Built in 1928 by the Wurlitzer Company of North Tonawanda, New York for the Stanley Theatre in Jersey City, the magnificent instrument had been a feature at a restaurant in Grand Rapids since the mid-1970s. It was slated for removal in 1991 when a group of local enthusiasts organized 'Operation Organ Transplant' to raise $187,000 to secure the Mighty Wurlitzer for the Museum's Meijer Theater. The effort was led by Beverly R. Howerton (RIGHT), long-time organist and Music Director for Fountain Street Church, shown here playing the instrument in 2004.

The G.M. Buck Pipe Organ Co. of Grand Rapids was hired to restore and install the organ, assisted by 20 community volunteers who contributed over 2,000 hours to the project. The Mighty Wurlitzer has become a favorite for concerts by professional artists, and as accompaniment to classic silent films and storytelling events.

powered, and a 1931 Driggs Skylark Biplane, made in Lansing and a rare survivor of the early days of aviation.

"When I became Director, a lot of input came from people—both formally and informally—about what the new Museum should be," reminisced Museum Director Timothy Chester in a 2004 interview. "I remember Fred Meijer took me aside and asked, 'Well son, where's the whale? Let me give you a piece of advice. Find that whale and put it in that new building.' And we did."

What Mr. Meijer knew, and was suggesting to the Director, was that certain objects represented the memory of the community. "It's not so much about natural history," explained Chester, "as it is about common identity. The meaning of the object changes because people have added their own meaning to it over time. A lot of stories got transmitted to Lawrence Man, the architect for the new building, and he really heard all the community's input. He studied old photos of how the whale was displayed in the old building, how you would have this sense of wonder right away as you came in the door, and he captured that sense of wonder, plus made it visible from the outside."

"The best thing, though, in that museum was that everything always stayed right where it was . . . You could go there a hundred thousand times, and . . . Nobody'd be different. The only thing that would be different would be you."

—Holden Caulfield
The Catcher in the Rye (J.D. Salinger, 1951)

The Evolution of Exhibitions

The opening of Van Andel Museum Center came on the crest of a wave of new interest in museums nationwide. Between 1989 and 1999, attendance increased at museums by nearly 30%, according to the American Association of Museums. But these new visitors had changing expectations of what a museum experience could be. With new travel and communication technology, the visible world had lost much of

BELOW: **Exhibits in the 'whale barn,' built in 1906 beside the carriage house of the original Kent Scientific Museum, were typical of 19th-century style 'parlor collection' displays.**

LEFT: **Interpretive exhibitions in the *Habitats* galleries at Van Andel Museum Center illustrate a transition to contemporary techniques, combining specimens collected by the Museum throughout its history with information that examines interrelated ecosystems.**

its mystery. Museum curators were challenged to create an experience to rival the multi-sensory, multi-disciplinary, short-attention-span fare to which the average American had become accustomed.

Contrary to the memories of Holden Caulfield, museums are now constantly changing and adapting to new ideas about the world and its people, and new understanding of material culture. Objects may remain in the collections for a long time, but the way they are exhibited has changed many times over the 150-year history of the Public Museum.

When Henry Ward came to Grand Rapids in 1922 as the new Director of the Kent Scientific Museum, he brought with him a radical new exhibition technique known as the habitat diorama. Developed at the Milwaukee Public Museum, where he had been Director from 1901-1922, the first total habitat diorama, The Muskrat Group, was created by Carl Akeley in 1890.

Ward was quick to introduce the innovation to the local Museum. Most of the exhibits in the mansion-turned-museum at the corner of Jefferson and State were of the old school: 'parlor collections' assembled by gentlemen of the 19th-century Lyceum of Natural History and Grand Rapids Scientific Club, displayed in large wooden and glass curio cabinets. In 1927, Ward and Museum Preparator E.A. Hyer embarked on a project to create five of the new

dioramas to depict Michigan mammals. According to a *Grand Rapids Herald* article, the pair found space for the new displays "by suppressing a considerable and valuable exhibit of ceramics and glass now filling 58 sugar barrels

Many media are used in creating an effective museum exhibition, from hands-on (or in) case work to a sophisticated computer system.

RIGHT: Gary Fraser, Exhibit Preparator and man of many Museum talents from 1974 to 2004.

BELOW LEFT: Tom Bantle, who came to the Museum during construction of the new building in 1992 and became Curator of Exhibitions in 1995, working at his computer in December, 2003.

BELOW RIGHT: Robert Bushewicz, Museum Artist and Chief Preparator from 1961 to 1980; and Milda Purins, Exhibitions Preparator 1955-1976, create exhibitions for the Hall of American Costumes in 1962.

in the basement and much mourned by many fanciers." The resulting groups were so lifelike that, according to the same article, "Many children have to be assured by their parents that the animals are not alive and will not hurt them before they will pass the door." More about the artistry of the early dioramas can be found in Chapter Four of this book.

For a very large portion of the Public Museum's history, one of the most important skills required for the preparation of exhibits was taxidermy. There are many interesting accounts in the Museum archives of forays into the Michigan wilderness to obtain specimens, and the talented people who constructed lifelike habitats in which to display them. The person most associated with those talents in the Museum's history, however, is Herman Hinrichs, who joined the staff of the Kent Scientific Museum in 1930.

A native of Iowa, Hinrichs began his career at age 20 with the Field Museum of Natural History in Chicago, where he also studied sculpture at the School of the Art Institute. After five years there, he came to Grand Rapids, and served as Preparator for the Public Museum until 1976. Among his many accomplishments was the development in the 1950s of a new technique to use plastic epoxy resin and glass cloth to make specimens more lifelike and

durable. He became nationally known as a sculptor, photographer, botanist, craftsman and artist, and was offered a position at the Smithsonian Institution in Washington, D.C. but stayed with the local Museum.

The Museum also earned national recognition for innovative exhibition techniques in the building opened in 1940, including display windows visible from the street, reminiscent of department store windows, and recessed display cases built into the gallery walls inside (more about the "Grand Rapids plan" Museum building can be found in Chapter Four of this book). That facility and the East Building addition acquired in 1958 allowed the Museum staff to create a wide variety of permanent and temporary exhibitions.

When planning began for a new Museum building, ideas about exhibitions were changing. In 1972, the museum world had been rocked by *Treasures of Tutankhamun* at the British Museum in London. Huge crowds waited in long lines and even camped out overnight for tickets. The spectacular exhibition of gold and jewels found in the tomb of an Egyptian boy

ABOVE: **Exhibits staff ca. 1980 in a light-hearted moment, from left, Gary Fraser, Carl Ulanowicz, Sam Pope, John Perschbacher, Dave Vandenbos, Bob Bushewicz, Dennis O'Connell, and Ardath Allen.**

LEFT: **Exhibition Preparator Herman Hinrichs puts finishing touches on the Moose Group in 1955.**

RIGHT: In 1989, robotic dinosaurs from Dinamation International in California were a hit at the Public Museum on Jefferson Avenue, a dramatic contrast between high-tech, state-of-the-art exhibition techniques and the increasingly inadequate old facility. After the splendid new Museum building opened downtown, the dinosaurs returned in 1996 for *Yikes!! They're Back*, featuring the robotic creatures in custom-made West Michigan environments. The saga continued in the summer of 2000 with *Dinosaur Families: The Story of Egg Mountain*. Cover from *On-The-Town* magazine by Art Melendez.

BELOW RIGHT: Visitors wait to enter the third-floor Lacks Family Changing Exhibition Gallery in 2000 to see *Mysteries of Egypt*.

The ambitious exhibition broke all previous attendance records, but didn't hold the title for long. In 2003 *The Dead Sea Scrolls* brought more than a quarter-million visitors to the city from all over the world.

king who had died more than 3000 years earlier set the stage not only for King Tut fever when the show toured the U.S. in the late 1970s, but for a new phenomenon in museum exhibitry: the blockbuster show.

In Grand Rapids, Museum staff had already seen what a 'blockbuster' show could do for community support of the institution. As early as 1934, when Frank DuMond set new attendance records with *The Dutch Exhibit* (covered in Chapter Three of this book), the power of popular appeal was apparent. In the Jefferson Avenue building, space for temporary exhibitions was limited, but the Museum managed to draw overflow crowds for *Dinomania* in 1989, the first of three wildly popular exhibitions featuring animated robotic dinosaurs. It was clear that

the new building must have space to accommodate large and demanding touring exhibitions—and that the Museum would again have the opportunity to take advantage of new ideas about how its collections were showcased in the new facility.

"The big innovation in our exhibition development at Van Andel Museum Center was the use of cross-disciplinary teams, not just designers," said Curator Christian Carron, who came to the city in 1988 as one of the first Museum staff hired specifically with the new facility in mind. "We worked with leading exhibition designers like Jim Sims (a consultant from the Smithsonian Institution) and PRD (The Planning, Research, and Design Group, Ltd., of Fairfax, Virginia, whose clients included the Carter Presidential Museum and the

National Museum of Natural History in Washington, D.C.) to bring new ideas about the meaning of exhibits to Grand Rapids."

The designers and consultants worked with a wide variety of community advisory groups and Museum staff. The exhibitions at Van Andel Museum Center "have been crafted for the needs of today's visitors," wrote Museum Director Timothy Chester in the Fall 1994 issue of *Museum* magazine. "While some displays, like *The Furniture City,* (are) brand new, others are updated versions of cherished installations that still work. Visitors to (*Streets of Old Grand Rapids*), for instance, will recognize its debt to the old *Gaslight Village*, but they will also experience a wonderland of historical imagination that more clearly reflects the past of Grand Rapids with all of its accomplishments and faults."

The first two temporary exhibitions at Van Andel Museum Center were local showcases, a hands-on exhibition from the nascent Grand Rapids Children's Museum, *Wee Like What Wee See*, and *Reynold Weidenaar: The Graphic Visions of Grand Rapids*, featuring art work about people and places around West Michigan. During its first summer, the Museum also stepped in to rescue the *Festival '95 Visual Arts Exhibition*, an annual community event that had been temporarily dislocated before finding its permanent home at the Grand Rapids Art Museum.

But the Museum officially inaugurated its splendid new changing exhibition gallery, funded by and named for the Lacks family, with its first major traveling show, *American Arts & Crafts: Virtue in Design*, from the Los Angeles County Museum of Art, in the summer of 1995.

What has followed has been a line-up of educationally rich, crowd-pleasing, and record-setting shows such as *Yikes!! They're Back*, the return of the robotic dinosaurs in 1996 (and *Dinosaur Families: The Story of Egg Mountain* in 2000); *Rainforest Adventure: The Gold, Jade & Forests of Costa Rica* in 1997; and *Mysteries of Egypt*, which shattered all previous records by attracting 134,000 visitors from November 1999 to March 2000. A bonus of the excitement surrounding the exhibition of

LEFT: **The 1997 exhibition** *Rainforest Adventure: The Gold, Jade & Forests of Costa Rica* **was a triumph for the Public Museum's exhibitions staff and the new Lacks Family Changing Exhibitions Gallery. More than 150 examples of rare pre-Columbian art from the** *Museo Nacional de Costa Rica* **were displayed in an elaborate rain forest environment created by the local staff that also offered an innovative educational aspect with the look and feel of a gigantic board game.**

BELOW: *Streets of Old Grand Rapids* **in Van Andel Museum Center is reminiscent of the old** *Gaslight Village* **section of the Jefferson Avenue building.**

ABOVE: In cooperation with the Israel Antiquities Authority, the Public Museum brought rarely seen fragments of the 2000-year-old Dead Sea Scrolls to Grand Rapids for a meditative experience, designed and constructed by the Museum's exhibition staff. The project, featuring extensive educational programming, drew international attention including an article in *The New York Times*, (INSET RIGHT).

OPPOSITE: Van Andel Museum Center, arrayed in holiday finery December 2003

Egyptian antiquities assembled by the Canadian Museum of Civilization from North America's top museums was the reappearance of objects from the Public Museum's own extensive Egyptian collections, including the long-beloved and newly conserved mummy Nakhte-Bastet-Iru and the forensic reconstruction of her face that now graces a spe-

cial Egyptian gallery at Van Andel Museum Center (see Chapter Three for more details).

The promise and potential of Van Andel Museum Center was truly made manifest in the spring of 2003 with *The Dead Sea Scrolls*, organized by the Public Museum in collaboration with the Israel Antiquities Authority. More than 235,000 people came from all over the world to see the exhibition that included fragments of 12 scrolls rarely seen outside Israel, as well as artifacts from the ancient settlement of Qumran located near the scroll discovery site, set in a context to highlight the story of the discovery, conservation, and publication of the text of the scrolls and their deep significance in today's world.

Attendance at the show ranked second in listings compiled by an international journal of all antiquities exhibitions staged world-wide that year, and earned

Grand Rapids international attention. An ambitious supplemental program of lectures, classes, forums, and academic meetings set a new standard of education and public programming at the Museum that continues to enhance the visitor's experience.

Although the project was not conceived for touring, it attracted immediate inquiries from other museums. "It looks like we're going into the traveling exhibition business," said Museum Director Timothy Chester in an April 2003 article in *The New York Times*. "We're a 149-year-old museum that has just reinvented itself." The exhibition will be presented at the Houston Museum of Natural Science in 2004 and the Gulf Coast Exploreum in Mobile, Alabama in 2005.

While exciting traveling exhibitions continue to bring crowds to Van Andel Museum Center, the Museum's own collections remain a primary source of fascinating and enlightening humanities and natural science exhibitions. Most of the permanent exhibitions at the Museum Center are continuously updated and improved as new artifacts are added to the collections, and an ongoing permanent exhibition titled *Collecting A–Z*, slated to be completed in 2004, has brought a myriad of extraordinary items into public view in a playful and visually lively series of displays grouped into alphabetic categories.

"Our exhibitions offer what TV and computers cannot," mused Curator Christian Carron in a 2003 interview, "the power of the object. As our daily lives become more virtual, the emotional experience of a personal encounter with the 'real thing' has become even more important. Museum exhibitions offer something that other media do not—evidence that provides a direct link between the past and the visitor."

As it moves into the second half of its second century, the Public Museum is maintaining that link by preserving that evidence and evolving its facilities and staff to continue to provide engaging community encounters with "real things" in many ways, the subject of the next and final chapter of this book.

9. Traveling Hopefully: 1994 and Onward

"To travel hopefully is a better thing than to arrive."
—Robert Louis Stevenson, 1881

When the Museum committee that coordinated the production of this book first began to meet in the fall of 2001, there was consensus on at least one point. The Public Museum of Grand Rapids has not arrived anywhere, except at a milestone on a continuing journey.

"The anniversary gives us the opportunity to stand back from the day-to-day world and see how we got to be a 150-year-old institution," said Larry Shay, President of the Grand Rapids Board of Art & Museum Commissioners, in a 2003 interview. "It's our responsibility to make sure it's here 150 years from now, and to think about the fundamental human needs this institution serves. I know they are fundamental, because we've been here 150 years. I can't say exactly what all those needs are, but first, you don't know where you're going if you don't learn where you've been. It's an insatiable need, a need to touch the continuity of human experience. John Ball and the group that started the Museum decided that they had that need. I recognize that I have that need. Very likely in 150 years people will have that need. It's a reassur-

ance that this whole life experience is more than just me.

"People come here for the past to be present in their lives," he continued. "The Dead Sea Scrolls were just tiny pieces of paper — if you saw them in a side hall of some large museum, you'd just walk right by. But the story we told was so powerful, it filled a human need to be in the proximity of the object."

Objects and the stories they tell continue to be the force that drives the Museum. In a 150-year history of ups and downs, comings and goings, budget cuts and generous gifts, thwarted plans and ambitious building projects, what endures quietly underneath it all is the

collection and its use for education and enrich-ment. The story of the Public Museum's collec-tion is also the story of its many dedicated peo-ple — staff, volunteers and community benefac-tors who keep the institution going through thick and thin. And, it's the story of the institu-tion's many buildings, a continuing progress of displaying the community's treasures to tell its ever-changing stories, while keeping those treasures safe and secure.

After the triumph of decades of work was realized in Van Andel Museum Center, one might think that the Museum would rest on its laurels for a few years. But, as Mary Jane

Dockeray so succinctly put it in Chapter Six of this book, to be in the museum business you have to be an opportunist — and when opportu-nity came knocking in 1998, the Museum once again was ready to rise to the challenge of a major building project, the culmination of nearly 150 years of evolving answers to a recur-rent question.

What Do We Do With This Stuff?

One of the biggest decisions about Van Andel Museum Center was not to put collections stor-

What do we save and where do we put it? When the splendid new Museum Center was opened in 1994 on the Grand River downtown, many beloved objects from past exhibitions were moved and reinterpreted with more con-temporary information. But some, including the Timber Wolves (ABOVE) and other dioramas originally created more than a half-century earlier (see Chapter Four), were preserved simply because they had become cherished icons of the community's memories of the museum.

age on-site. "That decision led us in a whole different direction," explained Timothy Chester, Director of the Museum, in a 2004 interview. "The original vision was that the top floor would be collections storage." He credits Jay Van Andel, chair of the building's capital campaign, with helping to clarify their thinking in an early discussion of plans for the riverfront site. "He asked us, 'Why would you put your warehouse in your most expensive real estate?'" remembered Chester. "It helped us put that in perspective, and also helped in our thinking about the old Museum building on Jefferson Avenue."

The Public Museum's collections have been housed in a wide range of facilities over the years. In the 19th century, most were held in private homes or stored in school buildings. In 1906, just two years after the first facility wholly dedicated to the Museum opened in a mansion on the corner of Jefferson & State, the acquisi-

tion of a large whale skeleton made it necessary to construct a long shed behind the house. The 'whale barn' served as a display area for the 70-ft. skeleton, as well as a variety of other objects and collections.

The whale barn was not dedicated to storage, however, and before long Director H.E. Sargent was feeling the pinch of inadequate space. In 1917 the Board of Art & Museum Commissioners agreed to rent another vacant mansion, the Hughart house directly across the street from the Museum at Jefferson and Island (now called Weston Street). The building became known as the Museum Annex, and housed collections display in thirteen rooms and halls, plus four precious storage rooms and closets.

The problem of collections storage could only get worse, as the avidly acquisitive Sargent and his successor Henry Ward, along with generous donors, added to the collections and dis-

ANNEX TO KENT SCIENTIFIC MUSEUM
Jefferson Avenue and Island Street; Opposite Main Building

plays until the two old mansions were stuffed to the rafters. Despite Ward's repeated and increasingly testy pleas to the City Commission for assistance, decades passed before any move was made.

In July 1931, the Board of Art & Museum Commissioners notified the City Commission that, according to *Grand Rapids Press* reports, "it must decline to accept further responsibility for any avoidable losses by fire and further deterioration of value due to storage because of lack of room." In the *Press* story, delightfully headlined "Details City Dads to Guard Relics," the communication from Commissioners Alfred W. Wishart, Emerson W. Bliss, Leslie A. Butler, John J. Smolenski, and Mrs. Florence Hills Waters is quoted. "We repeatedly have brought this matter to your attention in conferences and therefore have no other recourse but to place the responsibility for the above mentioned conditions upon your honorable body. We feel some action should be taken by you to protect this property of the citizens and taxpayers of our city by providing suitable adequate and fireproof accommodations for these collections."

Mayor John D. Karel referred the matter to an administrative committee, which responded by vacating the Weston Street Annex, closing the main mansion building, and signing a three-year lease on the Hart-Nash garage at the corner of State Street and Waverly Place, just southeast of the Museum.

The triumphs of Director Frank DuMond in the Museum's three-year stay in the old automobile garage, and its role as a source of inspiration for the design of a new Museum building at Jefferson and State, are chronicled elsewhere in this book. When construction of the new building began in 1937, many of the collections were stored at an unused school building. A large portion remained there until 1946, when Kensington School was slated to be re-opened. Following the lead of many businesses taking advantage of post-war surplus, a Quonset hut was purchased and erected in the Museum's 'backyard,' where it was used for storage until

1963 when it was hauled away to the city dump on Butterworth Avenue.

Frank DuMond and the Museum community continued to plead for adequate space to safely store the collections not on display in the new Jefferson Avenue building. In 1951, a *Grand Rapids Herald* article about crowded conditions lamented that a large tropical bird collection had to be burned — storage moths and extreme temperatures had ruined it. And the Museum's coin and currency collection had been stored for 25 years in a bank vault. The purchase in 1958 of the East Building, another old auto showroom, eased some problems, but with the addition of the Furniture Museum, Garden

LEFT: **Frank DuMond and Norma Raby work in the Museum's crowded Quonset hut in 1951. The prefabricated shelters were developed for quick shipping and assembly during World War II and first produced at a facility near Quonset Point, Rhode Island. At the end of the war they were sold to the public. The Museum's hut was hauled away in 1963 (ABOVE).**

OPPOSITE: **The first expansion of Museum facilities was to a mansion across the street from the original Museum building on Jefferson Avenue. It became known as 'the Annex'.**

ABOVE: While Museum administrators worked diligently to find a safe, secure storage facility, collections staff and volunteers made sure that artifacts were well cared for. Pictured here, Arlene Whittemore, Laura Lorenson, who became Curator of Exhibits in 1943 and served for nearly 20 years, and Mrs. R.H. Gilbert work on the textiles collection in 1961.

ABOVE RIGHT: Before the City purchased the East Building for the Public Museum, space was rented in what was then the Medical Arts Supply Co. for collections storage. Conditions, as illustrated in this 1957 photograph, were less than ideal.

Center, and Planetarium, there was little storage benefit to the acquisition.

Finally, in 1976, the building on State Street that had housed the Museum briefly during the Depression was purchased by the City for collections storage, the first dedicated solely to that function. The triangular two-story garage had most recently been a business called Wicker Village, and was commonly known by that name until it became universally tagged 'the Attic.'

"A museum may be likened to an iceberg," wrote Museum Director Weldon D. Frankforter in his 1976-77 annual report. "Only a small portion of its collections show, but the curating of those collections constitutes one of the most important aspects of museum work."

By the late 1970s, talk about a new Museum was rumbling louder. In 1983, the Museum for the first time opened its storage building to the public to dramatize the necessity for new facilities. More than 1,500 people toured 'the Attic'

during the annual Open House, wrote Director W.D. Frankforter in the annual report for that year. "They all seemed to go away with a better understanding of the problems facing the Museum with its inadequate, complicated and dilapidated storage facility." They also realized, continued Frankforter, "that the Museum indeed has many thousands of items that it is unable to display because of lack of exhibit space. A new Museum will help solve these problems and provide for the safe and perpetual care of the collections, which are really the tangible evidence of this area's history."

The new Museum was a long time in coming, however. Staff made do with the Attic and a number of other stop-gap measures, including space in the Weston fire station annex, where large vehicles, architectural fragments and other bulky items were stored, and nooks and crannies tucked away all over town in various city-owned facilities.

Finally, in 1987, using municipal funds freed by Kent County's offer to operate the John Ball Park Zoo, the City Commission committed to the purchase of a warehouse in downtown Grand Rapids for Museum collections storage, and challenged the community to raise $50,000 to cover the cost of moving more than 350,000 artifacts. A major fundraising effort at Woodland Shopping Center in the fall met the goal. The gala event centered around the display of one of the Museum's most prized collection items, the whale skeleton, which had been restored for the occasion (see Chapter Six).

It took two years to renovate the facility and complete the move from the State Street 'Attic' to the Star Building at 134 Grandville Avenue. Built in 1927 by the Star Transfer Line, it had most recently served as warehouse and headquarters for Beverly's Inc., a locally based chain of women's apparel stores. With more than 40,000 sq. ft., and amenities such as a loading dock, freight lift, and large storage areas on three levels, the structure also offered increased

security, fire protection, and more work space for staff and researchers, as well as convenient access to the new Museum site taking shape on the riverfront downtown. Many of the exhibitions for Van Andel Museum Center were planned and staged at the Star Building.

The collections were scarcely settled in their new home before the Museum was anticipating future needs. A federal grant funded a conservation survey in 1990, and development of a long-range Storage Master Plan. By March, 1995, just a few months after the opening of the new Museum Center, Collections Manager Marilyn Merdzinski wrote in *Discoveries* newsletter that the Museum "has extended an invitation to the Grand Rapids Public Library, the Grand Rapids Historical Commission, and the Grand Rapids City Clerk's office to join us as we explore the potential of developing a site where all of the publicly owned historical resources of the City of Grand Rapids could be gathered together under one roof for better storage and public access." She was writing about the former home of the Public Museum at 54 Jefferson SE.

Opportunity Knocks

In April 1998, Museum Director Timothy Chester announced that a collaborative team was researching the creation of a Community

2001 Terrorist attacks on World Trade Center in New York City, Pentagon in Washington, D.C.

2001 AOL/Time Warner merger largest in U.S. corporate history

2002 Euro becomes unified currency for many states in European Union

2002 Acclaimed sculpture park opens at Meijer Gardens in Grand Rapids

2002 Odyssey spacecraft finds evidence of water ice deposits on Mars

January 1, 2003 The Public Museum of Grand Rapids Friends Foundation established

2003 Grand Rapids Public Library re-opens in restored Ryerson/Keeler building

2003 DeVos Place Convention Center opens in downtown Grand Rapids

2003 Space Shuttle Columbia and seven astronauts lost on return to Earth

2003 U.S.-led invasion of Iraq ousts Saddam Hussein

2003 North America's worst electrical blackout affects more than 50 million

November 2004 Public Museum of Grand Rapids celebrates 150th birthday

TOP LEFT: Veronica Kandl, associate curator of history, and curatorial assistant Kate Molumby work on rehousing Native American artifacts in new specialized archival storage cabinets at the Public Museum's Community Archives & Research Center in 2001.

LEFT: Jeanne Larsen, Collection Management Office Assistant at the Museum since 1988, at the Star Building collections storage, ca. early 1990s.

Demolition began on the East Building on State Street in January 1999 (ABOVE, TOP), just 18 months before the destruction of the Star Building on Grandville Avenue to make way for the new U.S. 131 freeway (VISIBLE BEHIND THE BUILDING, ABOVE) in June 2000. Construction of the first phase of the Community Archives & Research Center, and the packing and transport of 197 semi-truck loads of Museum collections, happened in the interval.

first for the site of the former East Building, and a West Phase for the WPA-moderne building at 54 Jefferson and the Gaslight Village structure between the two.

Shortly after the plan was devised, Chester received a phone call. The Michigan Department of Transportation (M-DOT) was in the middle of final routing plans for reconstruction and improvement of the U.S. 131 expressway 'S-Curve' in downtown Grand Rapids. The most recent design ran right through the site of the Star Building, and M-DOT was calling to see if the Museum could vacate the building in 15 months. "I felt ill," wrote Chester in his October 1998 column outlining the process. "We completed paying off the loans for it … only last year! Only after I calmed down did the good news dawn on me. We would have to move out!" With compensation from M-DOT for the cost of relocating the collections into a new facility, it was possible to fast-track the first phase of the proposed Community Archives & Research Center (CARC) on Jefferson Avenue.

And fast-track they did. Demolition crews moved in at the old Museum site at the beginning of 1999, and by mid-July, 2000, the collection was safe in its new home. "The whole thing was overwhelming," mused Collections Manager Marilyn Merdzinski in the September 2000 newsletter. She credited her staff and the move contractor, Boston-based fine art-handling company FAE Worldwide.

Archives & Research Center. "With Grand Rapids City Manager Kurt Kimball, City Clerk Terri Hagerty, Kent County Clerk Terri Land, and Public Museum staff as joint planners," wrote Chester in his newsletter column, "a study committee has been formed chaired by Mary Esther Lee, the Museum's Planning and Development Officer." He outlined a process involving architectural consultants, a feasibility study, engineering studies, and conservation studies, to be completed by July 1. The result was an ambitious two-phase, long-term plan,

A New Era of Collections Management

The actual square footage of the first phase of the new facility, also housing city and county records and archives, was similar to the Star Building's storage capacity. But there the likeness ended. The new building, the Museum's first "purpose-built" storage facility, was designed with state-of-the-art climate control, access control, and other protective measures such as use of solvent-free paints. The Museum also utilized a number of grants from a variety of sources to upgrade specialized storage capabilities.

Along with increased physical capacity, the Museum has continued improvements in collections management and accessibility. In 1987 separate Collections Management and Curatorial Departments were organized, and the transition to an automated collections recordkeeping system was begun (the early records of the Public Museum's 150 years of collecting have become intriguing artifacts as well as archives).

"The role of collections storage is changing," said Collections Manager Marilyn Merdzinski in a 2003 interview. "It's moving toward a system where anyone can walk in and see anything that the Museum owns." It's a different way to operate, she acknowledged, but "we're heading to the best of both worlds — professionally created interpretive exhibitions, and access to collections of 'stuff' not interpreted." The latter alludes to a historic exhibition style described by Merdzinski, who started working at the Museum in 1977, as "line it up and let me look at it." The exhibitions at Van Andel Museum Center reflect the mix of styles. "There's an interpretive exhibit, such as *Habitats*, then an encounter with collections without much interpretation, *Y is for Yearlings* and *Z is for Zoology*," said Merdzinski. "At CARC we're hoping to take it a step further — people can come in and just see what we have, reminis-

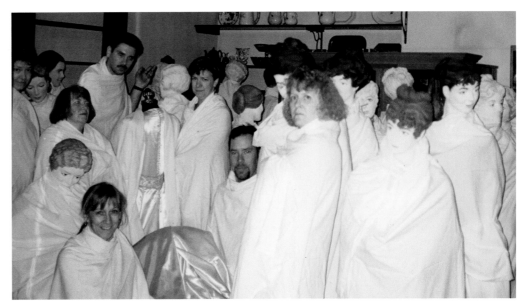

cent of the halls that used to be in the Jefferson Avenue building. We're also working on computer access — a shared electronic catalog for all partners."

As the development of the Community Archives & Research Center has evolved, the plan has been modified into three phases, with a budget nearing $20 million. The center structure that formerly housed *Gaslight Village* was demolished and new construction providing further storage and a public entry begun in the summer of 2003. Plans for the WPA-moderne Museum building at 54 Jefferson schedule renovation and development in 2005-06.

What is History?

In 1987 and 1988, when much about the Public Museum was undergoing growth and change, a new logo was introduced incorporating images from the Museum's major sites and representing "diverse Museum activities and locations that emanate from a single program philosophy, implemented by a unified staff," according to Director Timothy Chester's annual report.

In 2004, as this book was

ABOVE: **In the building that once housed Gaslight Village, linking the two wings of the old Museum, Collections staff pause for a humorous snapshot while reorganizing costume hall mannequins stored there, ca. 1994-95. From left, back, Renee Therriault, Diane Harwood, Christian Carron, Marilyn Merdzinski, Bryan Kwapil, Gina Bivins, and in front, Jeanne Larsen.**

LEFT: **Marilyn Merdzinski, Public Museum Collections Manager, taking the last ride in the summer of 2000 on the monorail train that once circled the basement of Herpolsheimer's Department Store in downtown Grand Rapids. In a 2003 interview, Museum Curator Christian Carron said that the train is a perfect example of an object that was collected because the community determined its relevance. Marilyn, as one of the many Grand Rapids native "baby boomers" who rode the Santa Polar Express around the toy department in the 1950s, took special delight in helping to collect and preserve a treasured community memory.**

ABOVE: Larry Shay, President of the Grand Rapids Board of Art & Museum Commissioners.

OPPOSITE: Large object storage at the Community Archives & Research Center, 2004.

being produced, a team of staff and consultants was again working diligently on a new public image for the Museum, reflecting the new Community Archives & Research Center, changes at Blandford Nature Center, the Norton Mounds Project, and ongoing work by Museum leadership in governance and organizational transformation. When this book is published in fall 2004, the logo that appears in its front pages will already be part of its history.

"The Public Museum is an organic institution — it changes and grows, it's alive," said Larry Shay, President of the Board of Art & Museum Commissioners, in a 2003 interview. "We expand, such as the Archives Center, and we spin off Blandford, which is better for our community. The world changes."

On January 1, 2003, the Museum's world changed substantially, with the formation of the Public Museum of Grand Rapids Friends Foundation, an organization created by the merger of the Friends of the Public Museum, established as the Grand Rapids Museum Association in 1952, and the Public Museum Foundation of Grand Rapids, established in 1988.

The idea of merging the two groups into a single organization had its genesis in the re-accreditation report received from the American Association of Museums in 1996. The report was very favorable, but praise for the Public Museum's accomplishments was accompanied by a suggestion that a review of governance would be timely. "The existence of two separate organizations with development-related mission statements has created much confusion in the minds of members, funders and the public," wrote Timothy Chester in his newsletter column. "It has mystified donors and community supporters, and has resulted in fractured giving and inadequate donor recognition." The merger process was not easy, and ended up taking nearly three years, but on December 31, 2002, the two non-profit entities were dissolved, and the Public Museum of Grand Rapids Friends Foundation became an official united organization, finally combining

development and membership functions.

By the beginning of 2004, the new group had completed organizational structure work, and developed a three-year plan of action. "Now that the creative scaffolding is in place," wrote Dale Robertson, President of the PMGR Friends Foundation, in the April 2004 newsletter, "we believe we've got the tools necessary to build a secure future." Although optimistic about the future of the organization, Robertson was realistic. "It's also crucial to remember that the Public Museum, like any institution, is subject to the vagaries of the environment in which it lives and works. To wax Dickensian for a moment," he wrote, "it's safe to say that we find ourselves on the cusp in both the best of times, and the worst."

In a case study of the process prepared by Museum Director Timothy Chester and Grand Valley State University Associate Professor of Social Work Martha Golensky, the pair wrote, "2003 has been a time of great triumph and trauma for the Museum. Following on the heels of the very successful Dead Sea Scrolls exhibition, the organization was forced to cut hours by two days a week and lay off half of the professional staff as a result of cutbacks in financial support, including a $1 million reduction in its appropriation from the City of Grand Rapids." Chester was buoyed by the actions of the new Friends Foundation, but also wrote, "the cumulative mixture of success, trauma, high levels of public visibility, sorrow, and energizing, high-impact work has been emotionally draining." The Museum returned to seven-days-a-week operation in May 2004.

Looking back on 150 years of highs and lows, accomplishments and setbacks, can be not only enlightening but invigorating. "We want to take this moment of reflection—looking backward and looking forward—to stick our heads up above the fray," said External Relations Manager Mary Esther Lee in a 2004 conversation. "We gather the strength of our past around us and step forward."

In a 1989 release, contemporary musician

and performance artist Laurie Anderson borrowed ideas from the early 20th century German writer and critical theorist Walter Benjamin in a song titled *Strange Angels* (dedicated to Benjamin). One character in the song asks another, 'What is history?' Anderson paraphrases a Benjamin passage describing a painting by Paul Klee, written in 1940:

> **History is an angel being blown, backward, into the future.**
> **History is a pile of debris.**
> **And the angel wants to go back, and fix things.**
> **To repair the things that have been broken.**
> **But there's a storm blowing—from Paradise,**
> **and the storm keeps blowing the angel, backward, into the future.**
> **And the storm, this storm,**
> **is called Progress.**

A pile of debris. Another and more often-quoted maxim about history comes from George Santayana — those who cannot remember the past are condemned to repeat it.

Perhaps we are destined to continue being blown, backward, into the future, but all we can see for certain is the pile of debris we've left behind in the past. There's much to be remembered and learned from that ever-growing pile, however, things of meaning and value that prepare us for the storm of progress. The Public Museum of Grand Rapids travels hopefully into its next 150 years, preserving for the community the stories and artifacts of T.S. Eliot's "time present and time past . . . both perhaps present in time future, and time future contained in time past."

Author's Note

BELOW: Emma Cole's 1901 book *Grand Rapids Flora* (see page 16), chosen by Julie Stivers as her favorite object in the Public Museum's collection.

Many thanks to Tim Chester, who convinced me to do this project, which was, as I predicted, a tremendous amount of work, but also, as he predicted, a truly fascinating and rewarding effort. Thanks also to the Museum staff team for the project, whose many ideas and suggestions brought about the synthesis of the book's structure: Chris Carron, Tim Chester, coordinator Veronica Kandl, Mary Esther Lee, Marilyn Merdzinski, and Beth Ricker. The Collections staff at the Community Archives & Research Center, especially Jeanne Larsen, were invaluable in making this book. Many thanks to all the helpful Public Museum staff and volunteers, especially Assistant Public Relations Officer Pete Daly. I am grateful to many people who helped me find images and information

for this book, including the staff at the Grand Rapids Public Library's History and Special Collections Center, especially Christine Byron and Rebecca Mayne; the City of Grand Rapids archivist William Cunningham; graphic designer Ruth Oldenburg; and the photography department at The Grand Rapids Press. My intrepid fact-checker Sue Fitzgerald saved me from several embarrassing date errors (any remaining are purely my own fault). Book designer and photographer Tom Kachadurian, who is also a skilled wordsmith, was a wonderful collaborator. Thanks also to my husband John, whose patience during this three-year process was perhaps partly due to the demands of his own book production project.

I also would like to join Tim Chester in dedicating this book to the thousands of hard-working staff and volunteers who have kept the Public Museum going for 150 years, through good times and difficulties. One fact shone through in the research for this book—they are amazing. Although we tried to include as many as we could in this history, unavoidably we have left out a large number whose contributions have been considerable. My apologies to them, and my thanks for their devotion.

About the Photographs

Unless otherwise noted, all images and objects are from the collection and archives of the Public Museum of Grand Rapids. Every effort has been made to contact photographers whose work can be identified, but many photographs in the Museum's archives are unmarked. Please contact the Public Museum of Grand Rapids for information about specific images. The page numbers on which a photographer's work can be found are noted below.

Bantle, Tom: 127 bottom

Bulthuis, Patricia: 105 top

Carron, Christian: 66 top

Colorama Studio: 74 top; 86

Corriveau, John: 30 left; 31 bottom left; 42; 61 all; 64 left; 69 middle; 78 left; 84 top; 87; 90 top; 116 bottom; 118; 125 top.

Cunningham, William: 126

Daly, Peter: 28 top left and bottom (also on cover); 31; 83

Gaines, John L.: 60 bottom

Grand Rapids Public Library, Courtesy of the Grand Rapids History & Special Collections Center, Archives, Grand Rapids, MI.: 11 top left; 14; 23; 90 bottom left

Hamilton, T.J. (Used with permission of The Grand Rapids Press): 120

Hebert, William: cover photo M

Jerkatis, James A.: 111 top

Kachadurian, Thomas: cover photos A, D, F, I, L, N, R; 6; 10; 13 left; 16 top; 20-21; 25 top; 29 bottom right; 33-35; 36 top left and right; 40 bottom; 45; 47; 56; 57; 59; 60 right; 67; 68; 69 bottom; 77 top; 79 middle and bottom; 92 top; 97 middle and bottom; 98; 99; 103; 108 bottom left and right; 109 bottom; 112 bottom; 113 top; 114 bottom left; 117 bottom; 119; 121; 128; 129.

Kandl, Veronica: 127 top

Lindburg, R.J.: 125 bottom

Manos, Constantine: 97 top

McLellan, David: 44

NASA: 70

Robinson Studio: 38 top; 50; 62 top right and top left; 65 bottom

Rooks, Dale: 26 top left

Tabert-Lind, Mary (Spectrum Health): 36 bottom

Thomaszewski, Thomas: 95 right

Vander Lende Photography Inc.: 48 bottom; 54 top left and bottom. Both images used with permission of The Weidenaar Portfolio, Inc.

Ward, Allen: 96 top

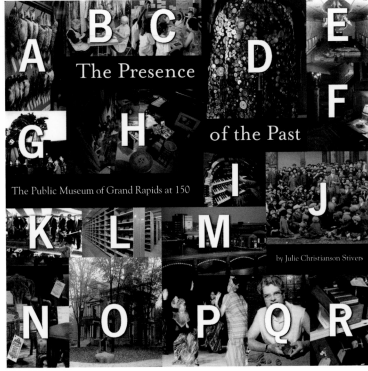

The Presence of the Past

The Public Museum of Grand Rapids at 150

The Furniture City, Van Andel Museum Center

by Julie Christianson Stivers

The Cover Photographs

A: Bird display in Kent Scientific Institute Room, Van Andel Museum Center.

B: Women sewing, see page 124.

C: Group at table, see page 28.

D: Button coat, see page 56.

E: Whale hanging above WPA-era topological maps in Jefferson Street museum.

F: Voigt House, see page 7.

G: Planetarium, see page 74.

H: *The Furniture City*, Van Andel Museum Center, see page 67.

I: Wurlitzer Theater Organ, Van Andel Museum Center, see page 112.

J: Group of students outside Kent Scientific Museum, see page 22.

K: Groundbreaking, Van Andel Museum Center, see page 106.

L: Sweeper storage, Community Archives and Research Center, see page 68.

M: Van Andel Museum Center at night.

N: Chairs in *The Furniture City*, Van Andel Museum Center.

O: Kent Scientific Museum, see page 17.

P: Dancers, see page 41.

Q: Mary Jane Dockeray, see page 77.

R: Lantern slides from education collection ca. 1890-1940, in storage, Community Archives and Research Center.

SOURCES

Alderson, William T., ed. *Mermaids, Mummies, and Mastodons: The Emergence of the American Museum.* Washington, D.C.: American Association of Museums, 1992.

Asma, Stephen T. *Stuffed Animals and Pickled Heads: The Culture and Evolution of Natural History Museums.* Oxford: Oxford University Press, 2001

Bahle, Jean Reed. *Invisible Journeys.* Unpublished play, 1994.

Ball, John. *Born to Wander.* Compiled by his daughters, Kate Ball Powers, Flora Ball Hopkins & Lucy Ball, 1925. Reprint. Grand Rapids: Grand Rapids Historical Commission, 1994.

Belknap, Charles E. *The Yesterdays of Grand Rapids.* Grand Rapids: The Dean-Hicks Company, 1922.

Burleigh, Nina. *The Stranger and the Statesman.* New York: HarperCollins, 2003.

Bredhoff, Stacey. *American Originals.* Washington, D.C.: National Archives and Records Administration, with Seattle and London: The University of Washington Press, 2001.

Carron, Christian G. *Grand Rapids Furniture, The Story of America's Furniture City.* Grand Rapids: The Public Museum of Grand Rapids, 1998.

Coleman, Laurence Vail. *Museum Buildings.* Washington, D.C.: American Association of Museums, 1950.

Dana, John Cotton. *The New Museum: Selected Writings by John Cotton Dana.* Newark and Washington D.C.: The Newark Museum Association and the American Association of Museums, 1999.

DuMond, Frank L. *A Narrative History of the Grand Rapids Public Museum, 1854-1970.* Unpublished manuscript, archives of the Public Museum. 1970.

Eliot, T.S. *Collected Poems 1909-1962.* London: Faber and Faber Limited, 1963.

Elliott, Gerald, with Ellen Arlinsky, Marg Ed Conn Kwapil, and Barbara McGuirl. *Grand Rapids: Renaissance on the Grand.* Tulsa: Continental Heritage Press, Inc., 1982.

Fitch, Geo. E., rev. and updated by James Van Vulpen and Gordon Olson. *Old Grand Rapids, A Picture Story of Old Conditions.* Grand Rapids: Grand Rapids Historical Society, 1986.

Grun, Bernard. *The Timetables of History.* New York: Simon and Schuster, 1982.

Hall, Donald. *String Too Short To Be Saved.* Boston: Nonpareil Books, 1988.

Hambacher, Michael, & James A. Robertson, Commonwealth Cultural Resources Group. *The Norton Mounds Site: A Description and History of a Prominent Cultural National Historic Landmark.* Report prepared for Public Museum of Grand Rapids, 2003.

Miriam R. Levin, "Museums and the Democratic Order." *The Wilson Quarterly,* v. 26, no. 1, Winter 2002.

Lively, Penelope. *The Presence of the Past: An Introduction to Landscape History.* Glasgow: William Collins Sons & Co., 1976.

Lydens, Z.Z., ed. *The Story of Grand Rapids.* Grand Rapids: Kregel Publications, 1966.

Massie, Larry B. *A Grand Adventure.* Grand Rapids: Grand Rapids Historical Society, with Heritage Media Corporation, 2001.

Jayne Merkel, "The Museum as Artifact." *The Wilson Quarterly,* v. 26, no. 1, Winter 2002.

Nabokov, Peter. *A Forest of Time, American Indian Ways of History.* Cambridge, United Kingdom: Cambridge University Press, 2002.

Newhouse, Victoria. *Towards a New Museum.* New York: The Monacelli Press, 1998.

Olson, Gordon L. *A Grand Rapids Sampler.* Grand Rapids: The Grand Rapids Historical Commission, 1992.

Bonnie Pitman, "Muses, Museums, and Memories." *Daedalus,* v. 128, Summer 1999.

Salinger, J.D. *The Catcher in the Rye.* Boston: Little, Brown and Company, 1951.

Samuelson, Linda, and Andrew Schrier, with others. *Heart & Soul, The Story of Grand Rapids Neighborhoods.* Grand Rapids: Grand Rapids Area Council for the Humanities & William B. Eerdmans Publishing Company, 2003.

Schwarzer, Marjorie. *History of American museums in celebration of the 100th anniversary of the American Association of Museums,* pre-publication manuscript. Washington D.C.: American Association of Museums, 2006.

Julian Spalding, "Museum Pieces." *History Today,* v. 52, No. 4, April 2002.

Van Vulpen, James. *Grand Rapids Then and Now.* Grand Rapids: Grand Rapids Historical Commission, 1988.

Vogel, Morris J. *Cultural Connections, Museums and Libraries of Philadelphia and the Delaware Valley.* Philadelphia: Temple University Press, 1991.

Weil, Stephen E. *A Cabinet of Curiosities: Inquiries into Museums and Their Prospects.* Washington and London: Smithsonian Institution Press, 1995.

—-. *Making Museums Matter.* Washington, D.C.: Smithsonian Institution Press. 2002.

INDEX